Also by Annie Choi

Happy Birthday or Whatever

SHUT UP, YOU'RE WELCOME

Thoughts on Life, Death, and Other Inconveniences

ANNIE CHOI

A TOUCHSTONE BOOK
Published by Simon & Schuster
New York London Toronto Sydney New Delhi

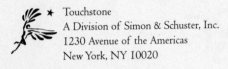 Touchstone
A Division of Simon & Schuster, Inc.
1230 Avenue of the Americas
New York, NY 10020

First Touchstone trade paperback edition July 2013

TOUCHSTONE and colophon are registered trademarks of Simon & Schuster, Inc.

For information about special discounts for bulk purchases, please contact Simon & Schuster Special Sales at 1-866-506-1949 or business@simonandschuster.com.

The Simon & Schuster Speakers Bureau can bring authors to your live event. For more information or to book an event contact the Simon & Schuster Speakers Bureau at 1-866-248-3049 or visit our website at www.simonspeakers.com.

Designed by Aline C. Pace

Manufactured in the United States of America

10   9   8   7   6   5   4   3   2   1

Library of Congress Cataloging-in-Publication Data
Choi, Annie
  Shut up, you're welcome : thoughts on life, death, and other inconveniences / Annie Choi.—First Touchstone trade paperback edition
      pages   cm
1. Choi, Annie—Humor. 2. Korean Americans—Biography. 3. Immigrants—United States—Biography. I. Title.
  CT275.C5725A3 2013
  974.7'1004957092—dc23
                                    2013005230

ISBN 978-1-4516-9839-8
ISBN 978-1-4516-9840-4 (ebook)

Dear Mike,

This book is dedicated to you.

Love,
Annie

Contents

Dear Musical Theater,

Let me be frank: I do not understand you.

I do not "get it."

I'm deeply confused and possibly offended.

Theoretically, musical theater is something I should understand. For one thing, I understand music. As you know, I play in an indie rock band that's so indie and so edgy, we haven't even heard of ourselves. I'm also classically trained in piano and flute as well as a traditional Korean instrument called a *gayageum.* Its strings are thick and tough, and whenever I played too much, I got blood blisters. Question: How many people do you know who can shred on an instrument that dates back to the sixth century? Answer: Only one. That'd be me. So, really, I understand music. One might even say I'm a connoisseur; just check out my Deep Purple collection. In case you didn't know, Deep Purple wrote songs about trucks. In space.

I, of course, understand theater. Someone talks and then someone else talks back. Then one of them yells or sobs. Most of the time, they do both. One of my friends has been involved with a number of avant-garde plays that explore different topics but always feature nudity. Those have been pretty good, I guess. They would've been better had they starred Captain Jean-Luc Picard (fully clothed). I know that if the play is by Shakespeare, there are a lot of words like "thine" and "hast" and questions like "Do you bandy looks with me, you rascal?" If it's by Mamet, there are questions like "You think this is abuse, you cocksucker?" I enjoy theater because it asks the questions we ask ourselves every day.

So yes, I understand music and I understand theater. But put them together and it becomes a riddle wrapped in a mystery stuffed inside an enigma, served with a side of trombones. Seventy-six of them to be exact.

I'm not sure why I don't get it. It all seems so simple in concept: Something happens, something else happens, then another thing happens, and then curtains close, applause, applause. Then we get out of our seats and wonder if we should take a cab home or take the subway. Boy meets girl, boy and girl fall in love, their families don't approve, the families fight, blah blah blah. Oh no! There is death! Sad face. The end. Taxi! It's all very classic. You can't go wrong with classic—that's why I have four black sweaters. But the problem is the singing. And the sheer amount of it.

It's not subtle singing either. The entire cast belts it out; their vocal cords are practically bursting through their O-shaped mouths. And the voices! They're piercing or booming or breathy or deep or nasal or raspy, and with plenty of vibrato. Words are so annunciated that every syllable gets its own solo, its own spotlight: *"Oak-ka-la-ho-ma, oh-kay!"* The high notes last forever. And ever. And they keep going until the audience starts clapping. They wipe tears from their eyes—oh, that was so magical! I'd like to remind you that there's no such thing as magic.

But wait! There's more! There's dancing that goes along with this singing. There are jazz hands and spirit fingers. There are pirouettes and tap-dancing, shuffle-ball-change, ta-da! There is skipping, sashaying, swooning. At some point someone leaps and does the splits in the air and touches his toes. It's almost always a guy, because it's impressive when a guy can touch his toes. The ladies get twirled around and lifted up. Sometimes by the crotch.

Let's not forget the acting. There are big, fake grins and wide, gleaming eyes. There are gaping mouths to show horror! Surprise! Disgust! Flailing arms to show humor! Frustration! Outrage! There are plenty of overzealous jumps for joy with overzealous cheering, hip-hip-hooray! Who even says that anymore?

Perhaps what's most confusing is the combination of dialogue with singing and dancing. There's talking and talking and then you feel the conversation build up to something and then slowly the music sneaks in and there's this sense of *Oh my God, everyone, we are about to sing a rousing number, get ready for a kick line,* and then soon people are singing while falling in love or dying or teaching a valuable lesson about life or wondering how to solve a problem like Maria, which is quite an awful thing to say, especially when it comes from a bunch of nuns. Nuns. A musical starring nuns. You can see why I might be puzzled. Why sing when you can talk? Why dance when you can just wave your hand once or twice?

What I simply can't get over are the ridiculous segues into songs: "Well, partner, let me tell you a little story, and it goes a little something like this . . ." (cue music). No, no, this won't do. Any writer, editor, teacher, or lover of English will tell you that the transition doesn't work; it's clunky and lazy. Plus in real life, no one ever introduces a little story that goes something like this—and then sings. There are rules and conventions we all follow. Without them it's chaos, which is why at this very second there's a pompous ass named Joseph singing about how his coat has so many amazing colors.

I do know people who enjoy musicals. I even know people who star in them. They're all upbeat and enthusiastic and kindhearted, and they're the people who show up to every performance, reading, or event I've ever been involved with, no matter how painful it is. I'm going to generalize here and say they are among the most loyal people I know and perhaps have the highest pain threshold. But I just don't feel the way these people feel about song and dance. Maybe something is dead inside of me.

Listen, if a guy came up to me wearing a white mask and wanted us to be lovers, I would Mace him. I would kick him while he was down, steal his wallet, and make fun of his cape. Oh yes, I would do all of this. Here's what I wouldn't do: break into song.

If an absurdly wealthy and very bald man wanted to adopt an adorable redheaded girl, I would say, "Good for you, ace! That's great. But please, don't sing about it." Angelina Jolie and Brad Pitt have adopted at least a hundred children, but they never sing about it. I think we can all agree that this is a good thing.

If a group of cats were whining in an alley and prancing around the garbage cans, I'd have them spayed or neutered. I like cats, I really do. So imagine what I'd do if I didn't like them.

I am 99 percent positive that Eva and Juan Perón did not sing to the people of Argentina.

What I'm trying to say here is that I'm confused. And perhaps this confusion is leading to some stronger emotions. Like rage. But I want to understand. When I watch a musical, I want to think, *Oh, this is what it's all about*. I do not want to feel hate. Or disgust. I want the pain to go away.

So please explain yourself. You can start by answering this question: What the fuck?

Your friend,
Annie Choi

BRAND-NEW STATE

I think my dad is gay.

But I'm not sure.

He does exhibit many of the stereotypical signs. For example, he adores Barbra Streisand. He owns several of her studio and live records, and he even has "best of" compilations that include songs he already owns ("But now all song in one place!"). This seems pretty gay to me, though I could be wrong. My father's been known to sing "The Way We Were" at karaoke with varying degrees of success, depending on your definition of success and, for that matter, singing. When he tries to nail the high notes, his face contorts and his eyes roll back into his head. It looks like he's caught his leg in a bear trap.

In third grade, I got a songbook of "favorite contemporary" ballads and I learned to play "The Way We Were" on the piano. My father was pleased. He'd stand in the living room and listen to me practice, singing along softly, lost in the plaintive, longing music. Then he'd cut in at the slightest mistake.

"No, Annie. Stop."

"Why?"

"Start over." My dad reached over and flipped the pages back to the beginning.

"But I'm playing it right!" I looked over the music. Quarter notes, half notes, whole notes, I knew them all like old friends. There were even lyrics under the notes so I could sing along or, more accurately, follow as my dad sang along, which took the guesswork out of the rhythm.

"Play it with feeling."

"I *am* feeling!"

"You need *more* feeling! Play from here!" He thumped his fist against his chest. "It's a love song, you understand? Feel it!" He shook his head at my injustice to Streisand, to love, and to anyone who had ever loved. Ever. "What do you love, Annie?"

"Now and Laters." Ah, those heavenly, sticky squares of joy that yanked every single filling out of my mouth. I liked eating the strawberry and the banana ones at the same time. A gourmand at age eight.

My dad frowned. "Barbra Streisand not sing about candy. She sing about love! What do you love?"

"I love unicorns."

"What?"

"You know, the white horses with the horn." I pointed to my forehead. One of my prized possessions was a purple and pink unicorn calendar. It was already two years old.

"What about me? Do you love Daddy?"

I shrugged. "Sure."

"You sure?"

"Yeah."

"Really?"

"Yes, yes, I love Daddy."

"Okay, then play for you daddy. *Feel* it!" He clutched his stomach tightly. "From here!" He thumped his chest. "From here!" He waved his arms wildly. "Feel it everywhere, you understand? You have to *believe* it." Apparently, my father missed his calling as a Method acting coach. De Niro could learn a thing or two.

In the end, I played the song really, really slowly because that's what I thought love was supposed to feel like. Slow and painful. A little boring. It was a very easy piece to play, much easier than Mozart or Beethoven, and eventually my mother told me to stop playing it for that very reason.

That same songbook had the music to "Aura Lee" and my father was tickled pink. He thought I was playing "Love Me Tender" by Elvis even though I was actually playing an old Civil War ballad. I tried to explain this to him and even read him the "About This Song" feature in my songbook, but he didn't care. He insisted on singing the Elvis lyrics and got cross when my version ended short. ("Play longer!") This song was even easier than the Streisand, and finally my mother tossed out the songbook and replaced it with a thick volume of Bach that forced me to explore both sides of the piano and actually use the black keys.

"No more Streisand. No more Elvis. You understand?"

"But it's not Elvis!"

She shook her head. "I know Daddy like, but it make me sleepy."

Just like that, she squashed my future as a lounge piano player. It was a sad day for my dad. I'm sure at one point he imagined me playing in a dark, smoky bar with a saucy dame draped on top of my grand piano. She'd be clad in a tight, red-sequined gown and crooning into one of those old-fashioned microphones that look like a car muffler. This dame might or might not be a drag queen. Meanwhile, my mother feared I'd end up at Bloomingdale's playing beneath the escalators, taking requests from shoppers. "'Wind Beneath My Wings'? Why, of course!"

But really, does loving Streisand and lounge piano really make my father gay? It's persuasive evidence but hardly decisive. Plenty of people, gay, straight, and everything in between, love Streisand. Even my grandmother loved *A Star Is Born*. But then there is my father's love of musicals.

My dad owns dozens of soundtracks, all by the original casts—*West Side Story, Evita, South Pacific, The Phantom of the Opera,* to name a few. I once thought I was named after the musical *Annie,* but my father explained my name had nothing to do with the show—besides, it debuted after I was born. Had I been a boy, my parents would've named me Robert, after Robert Redford. My mother insists that they weren't going to name me after the actor, they just really liked his name and they also really liked the actor. I failed to see the distinction. My brother Mike is named after Michael Caine. But that's beside the point. My dad adores musicals, it's as simple as that. His collection of soundtracks spans decades and is a veritable museum of technology. He has music in nearly every form: vinyl, eight-track, cassette, and CD. I found them all when I helped my parents move several years ago. My father balks at my mother's innumerable Catholic tchotchkes, but he has his share of detritus from the Golden Age, which, according to Wikipedia, began in 1948 and ended in 1968 with the musical *Hair.*

"Dad, do you need to keep this?" I held up the soundtrack to *Oklahoma!*

"Pack it up."

"Why? You'll never, ever listen to it. You don't even have a reel-to-reel player."

"I keep for the memory."

"Oh? What memory is that?"

"Annie." His eyes were stormy; he practically zapped bolts of lightning at me. Zzt.

"Fine. Fine." I sifted through more of his albums, something I hadn't done in fifteen years, maybe more. He owned an impressive assortment of Rodgers and Hammerstein as well as Andrew Lloyd Webber. "You own the soundtrack to *Starlight Express*? Is that the one with the roller skaters?"

My dad shrugged. "Not very good."

"You don't say."

"Annie." Zap, zap. Zzt.

"Okay, okay, I'll stop. Whatever." I threw the *Gypsy* soundtrack into a box and stifled a groan.

In high school, I played flute in the band (read: big nerd) and we were a part of the accompaniment for every musical (read: big pain). Over months of rehearsals I watched the school diva and divo belt out "Till There Was You" in the school production of *The Music Man*. It was torture, with bolo ties and suspenders. There weren't enough musicians in the orchestra, so the song "Seventy-Six Trombones" sounded more like "Two Trumpets and a Trombone Play Loudly to Compensate." The cast complained about the orchestra's playing; we complained about their singing. One star stormed off the set in tears. A stage mother threatened to pull her donations from the Theater Boosters. Everyone was outraged. The show is about a man who spreads his love of music. The whole thing was abusive and I should've pressed charges.

A few years ago my friend had an extra ticket to *Rent* on Broadway and dragged me along. Erin pulled me into the theater, commanded me to sit, and threw a *Playbill* at me. In the final act, she was dabbing her eyes as I was rolling mine.

"Listen, if you don't pay your rent, you're going to get evicted. It's New York fucking City! It's the Lower East Side!"

"They were making a stand." Sniff, sniff.

"Let me move in there. What was that, like, twelve hundred square feet? I'll totally pay my rent. I'll pay the living shit out of it. On time and everything."

"But it's not about that." Erin wiped her nose.

"Yeah, yeah, I know. Survival, friendship, love, blah, blah, blah."

"You can't even appreciate it? Just a little?"

"They were *singing* in *leg warmers.*"

I'm not even sure why she asked me in the first place, but Erin has never invited me to a musical again. Mission accomplished.

My father's favorite musical is *The Sound of Music.* When Christmas rolls around, he relaxes in his threadbare pajamas and watches it on TV even though he actually owns a copy and could watch all one hundred and seventy-four exhilarating minutes whenever he wants to without commercial breaks. He still cracks up at the scene when the nuns sheepishly hold up parts they pillaged from the Nazi jeep, allowing the Von Trapp family to escape. He's a big fan of Julie Andrews. According to one of my gay friends, she is "the gayest, most important nongay gay icon of the gay community. For real. Shut up, Annie, I'm being serious!"

When I was nine, my father gathered the whole family around the VCR and introduced us to *Mary Poppins.* To this day, it's the only musical I could conceivably consider liking. You'd have to be one callous, puppy-killing war machine not to love Mary and Bert when they tap-dance with animated penguins. Even my brother liked it, despite the lack of machine guns and explosions. I think my dad gets a little choked up at "Feed the Birds (Tuppence a

Bag)." I don't see the tears, but I know they are there. I can sense them building up during the song's melancholic phrasing.

All things considered, *Mary Poppins* went over well in our household, so my dad brought home another musical to share. Surely, he thought, we would all love this one as much as he did. It was *Seven Brides for Seven Brothers*, a musical set in the Old West starring Howard Keel and men in suede chaps. Each of the seven brothers wore a different-colored blouse, not unlike a boy band. They leaped and sashayed while cutting firewood and sang about parading into town and whisking away young ladies to take them as wives. It's obvious that they had no real interest in ladies, but that's why we call it acting. When you really think about it, the musical is actually about kidnapping and Stockholm syndrome. It's also about beards, both the literal and figurative kinds.

But maybe my father's love for musicals doesn't really make him gay. After all, I know plenty of gays who somehow loathe musicals more than I do, and I know plenty of straights who've raved about *Wicked*. I know better than to stereotype and generalize about an entire community and my dad, but it's exciting to think of my father as being different from the person I know. I've known him all my life, so wouldn't it be thrilling if I discovered something new? We'd have so much in common if he were gay. He would no longer be the alien chemist tooling around in his lab doing things I'll never fully understand or even try to.

One thing is for certain: My dad is gay for gardens. But gardens are universally loved by everyone—Adam and Eve loved them so much they lived in one. My father's lab is near Forest Lawn Memorial-Park and Mortuary, and whenever we drive past it he points out the cemetery's outstanding landscaping. I have been driving past this place with him for over fifteen years now, and he still looks at it in awe.

"Look! Look! How green is that grass!"

"It's nice."

"So thick! How do they make grass so thick?"

"It's the dead people. Good fertilizer."

He cringed. "Annie, no."

I should note that I have been telling this same joke for over fifteen years and my father still doesn't find it funny. One day he will, I'm sure of it.

"Look at the flower too! So pretty! Wow." You'd think he'd never seen that many flowers in his whole life. Except he saw them yesterday on his way to work. I admit it's admirable that he's kept this sense of awe and wonder about the same old place he sees every day, even if it is a cemetery.

"It's nice, Dad. Very flowery."

"What kind of flower you think?"

"It's too far away to see. I don't know. They're, uh, white flowers."

"I think carnation."

"Yeah, carnations sound good."

"Maybe lily?"

"Sure, dead people really like lilies."

My father spent a lot of time tending to his garden when Mike and I were little. He planted pansies, roses, and snapdragons, as well as apple, plum, and peach trees. He even planted a persimmon tree, at my mother's request. He was growing something in every single square inch of the backyard. I should say that he was *trying* to grow something. California's dry, desert heat, he discovered, was good for some plants but not for most of them. For example, watermelon doesn't grow well in the desert.

Every Saturday afternoon after Korean school, Mike and I had to weed the backyard. My dad thought it was fun. We thought it was child labor.

"Oh no! What you doing?"

"I'm weeding."

"Annie, that not weed! It iris!"

"No, it's not, it's a weed."

"Iris. Purple flower."

"Dad, it isn't purple, and it isn't a flower. It's green. So it's a weed." When you're in third grade, everything without petals looks like a weed.

"Put it back."

"I can't."

"Why?"

"Because the roots are still down in the ground. They broke off." I held up the iris-weed, which I had hacked off at the bottom.

"How many time I tell you, when you pull weed you have to pull out root. Or else it grow back!"

"Okay, so now it'll grow back!"

Whenever I walk past a garden, I don't marvel at its beauty or study its colorful plantings. I don't stop and smell the roses either. I just think of all the sweat and tears and unbelievable whining it took to care for every bud, leaf, and shrub. Then I watch for bees, which I'm allergic to. My brother thinks we should pave over everything just so no one has to mow anything. ("We'd save a lot of water, too. You think I'm joking?")

In addition to musicals and gardens, my father adores epic Roman period pieces of the silver screen. Specifically, he loves *Ben-Hur* and *Spartacus*. Bronze, bare-chested men with sculpted arms and chiseled abs, writhing and glistening in the light filtering through the columns of the Colosseum. Does this make him gay? Perhaps. I was about ten when I first watched *Ben-Hur* on double VHS cassette with my dad. I ate it up. I really wanted a chariot. White with gold trim, pulled by spectacular black stallions.

"A chariot is better than our car," I proclaimed. We had a death trap of a station wagon that choked and coughed up smoke whenever the engine started, causing us to choke and cough.

"Then Ben-Hur be our chauffeur!" My dad was lost for a minute. Tan, sinewy Charlton Heston snapping the reins. The wind blowing through our hair. And through Charlton Heston's leather skirt.

"Let's get one!"

"Ask you mommy."

My mother said no. Chariots don't have enough trunk space for groceries, she explained, plus, parking would be a torture.

"But not like the torture Ben-Hur went through." I nodded gravely.

My mother waved me off. She's always been more of a Gary Cooper kind of broad anyway.

On one weekend, my father ushered the whole family, plus Grandma, into the death trap and stole us away to Hearst Castle, the place where *Spartacus* was filmed. My brother and I would've preferred to visit a *real* castle, i.e., the one at Disneyland. But no. We went to Hearst Castle, a punishing five-hour drive away.

"Look at the ceiling! It twenty-four-karat gold. Can you believe it?"

"My neck hurts."

"Look at the statue! That marble!"

"He's naked! They're all naked!" I giggled, which was to be expected since I was ten. "Didn't they wear clothes at Hearst Castle?"

"Yes they wore clothes, stupid." My brother poked me. At thirteen, he was an impatient know-it-all. Which is to say, a dick.

"Mooommm . . ."

"Mike. Stop." My mother stared him down.

"What? I didn't do anything."

"Look, Annie, this is pool from *Spartacus!*" My dad smiled, no doubt recalling Crassus lounging poolside in his toga, laughing maniacally at those pitiful slave rebels.

The pool was stunning. The water was still and clear, like a flawless sheet of thin glass. I needed to shatter it. Destroy it. Conquer it and make it mine.

"Annie, what you doing?" My mother looked at me warily.

"Untying my shoes."

"Why?"

"So I can put my feet in."

"You're not allowed to swim in the pool, stupid." Mike pointed to a sign.

"Mooommmm . . ."

"Anne, keep shoe on. No swim."

"But can I go later?"

"No."

"Dad, can I go later?"

"No." My dad looked sad, a little wistful. To come this far and not be allowed to swim in the same pool as Sir Laurence Olivier? It was a shame, really, a damn shame.

Looking at photos of Olivier now, I can understand my dad's attraction. Olivier was a brooding dreamboat with the world's most perfect dimple in his powerful, well-defined chin. And you could get lost for days in those eyes. My father, mother, and I share the same taste in men. We love Cary Grant, Rock Hudson, and Gregory Peck. We think Jimmy Stewart is a very irresistible gentleman. According to my father, he's almost as irresistible as Danny Kaye.

In fifth grade, my teacher assigned James Thurber's "The Secret Life of Walter Mitty" and my father immediately rented the film version starring Danny Kaye. My father didn't know that the script had been adapted from a short story. Heavily adapted, which is a nice way of saying entirely changed. As far as I remember, the only common element was that there was a man named Walter Mitty. I described the differences and my dad was mortified. That short story, he explained, would've been a lot better if Danny Kaye were in it. I thoroughly enjoyed the movie and was willing to forget that Danny Kaye was a song-and-dance man (*White Christmas* is my dad's second-favorite musical). During the discussion in class, I explained quite haughtily that the movie was "way better," but no one seemed to care because no one in fifth grade knew who Danny Kaye was, though my teacher Mr. Rokke was pleasantly surprised. Most kids were watching *Robocop*, while I was watching a guy who daydreamed to escape his haranguing boss and nitpicking mother.

I once shared my thoughts about my dad's gayness with my brother, and he laughed.

"Dude, he's not gay, he's just an old FOB."

"Fresh off the boat" can be really demeaning to immigrants or American-born children of immigrants. But it can also be used with a lot of love and understanding and solidarity. Mike and I are quite intimate with the ways of the FOB—from the nonsensical "Engrish" on our Korean tracksuits to the eight-week-long SAT prep courses.

My parents immigrated here in 1971, a little before the Korean community in Los Angeles really exploded. They really were fresh off the boat, but my dad likes to say they were "pioneer, just like everybody in *Oklahoma!*" Like Curly, Laurey, and Aunt Eller, my parents moved to the West, to a "brand-new state / Brand-new state gonna treat you great." There was "wavin' wheat" and wind coming down the plains and something about a surrey with the fringe on top. Except their surrey was a tiny red Honda hatchback.

They nicknamed it "the Cherry." Then they got an Oldsmobile they nicknamed "the Lemon" because it was yellow. They didn't know the other definition of "lemon," which was also a fitting description of the Oldsmobile. Later, they got a station wagon, a Ford Country Squire. They didn't give it a nickname, though my mother did call it "a mistake."

When they settled in the San Fernando Valley, my parents were the only Korean couple in the neighborhood for several years. Everyone assumed they were Chinese or Japanese and when they explained they were from Korea, they got blank stares. But my parents forged ahead. My father worked as a chemist for a petroleum company, and my mother worked as a data processor, which is a nice way of saying she typed stuff that she didn't necessarily understand into a computer. They were on their way to fulfilling the American dream, the one people always mention when they talk about immigrants, the one dozens of musicals are about.

When my brother was born, they were living in a small one-bedroom apartment off a busy Valley thoroughfare. By the time I came around, they had saved up and bought a house with an overactive avocado tree in the front yard, which probably sparked my father's interest in gardening. Dark, squishy avocados fell and rotted on our lawn, attracting a flurry of insects. We didn't know what to do with them. There are only so many avocados a person can eat. And that person was my mother, because she was the only one of us who liked them. When she discovered how much fat was in them, she was mortified (thirty grams of fat, as much as a quarter-pound burger). She started mashing them up and smearing them on her face like a moisturizing mask, and, wouldn't you know it, the woman has fantastic skin. I think this taught me a little something about America: Everything grows well here, fruits, vegetables, flowers, children, so you're free to be creative with the excess, even if that excess causes your front lawn to smell like a jockstrap.

There were no Korean markets in the Valley, so my grandmother in Seoul shipped over a box of food every month, along with recipes. Now there's a behemoth supermarket on every block where you can buy Korean groceries, Korean movies, and Korean cosmetics, which include several types of skin whiteners. You can get Korean-style Chinese food, Korean-style Japanese food, and Korean-style fried chicken. You can also get a giant bowl of shaved ice with red bean, green tea ice cream, gummy bears, kiwi, and Fruity Pebbles. With a cherry on top. It's tasty, but it's a serious belly bomb. My dad often marvels at the Koreanness of Los Angeles with pride—"We here first!" He points at the new Korean banks or the karaoke bars, remembering what was there before. Then he drives right past all the Korean restaurants to get a foot-long roast beef sub. He eats Korean food every night; why not change it up for lunch?

In the early eighties, my grandmother stopped sending us food, and eventually she immigrated here to start all over again in her twilight years. Then the rest of our relatives followed. My parents had already blazed a path in the West, cleared the brush, so it was easier for everyone else. My father sponsored most of our relatives, and when they arrived in the States, they each stayed with us for a few months while they got the lay of the land and found new places to call home. Our family in America doubled and then tripled in size. We shopped at Costco. Everyone tried avocados and was unimpressed, but then fell in love with Royal Dansk butter cookies—the ones in the blue tin—for reasons I have never understood. They taste like margarine-flavored sawdust. It's a FOB thing. We swam in our pool together and had Korean barbecues. My mother introduced everyone to English muffins and bagels with cream cheese.

The immigrant pride and dreams of my father come out through his allegedly gay passions. Those epic Roman period pieces he loves showcase the glitz and glamour of America. They announce to the world that here in America, you have an opportunity to stage a stunning chariot race and re-create the Colosseum. Here in America, you can gild your ceilings in twenty-four-karat gold just because it looks fucking cool. Here in America, musicals are vibrant spectacles with sweeping scores and lavish set pieces, even when they feature dancing cats in spandex. His beloved Barbra Streisand sings about hope and love and longing, and who can't relate to that? It's Streisand! She is America's sweetheart, along with Shirley Temple and Judy Garland, whom my dad also adores. The idea that America is the land of opportunity seems too idealistic, simplistic, and optimistic to me. But this is the version of America my father lives and believes in.

My dad has the same conviction that every immigrant and, really, every American has—hard work, hope, and determination will lead you to happiness. His favorite movies and musicals and singers all explore the same theme: With enough resolve, you'll find love and freedom. You'll get the girl or the entire kingdom. You'll lead rebel slaves. You'll escape the Nazis. You'll befriend a chimney sweep. You'll be able to plant a garden with whatever you want because you have the space, though maybe not the green thumb, and your kids will get sunburned when you force them to mow the lawn. Your dog will keep the neighbors up. Things will be tough at times.

It'll be okay if your house smells different from every house on the block. It'll be okay if in your garage, there are jars of spicy squid pickling under thick layers of scum with a sour stench so bad that it brings shame to your kids and keeps them from inviting friends over. Then they will grow up and realize it's the most delicious thing they can shove down their face holes, and then later they will rebel and turn vegetarian. But no matter how many Sharks or Jets chase you down or how many mountains you must climb, you'll find a way to break out into song, and when the curtains close, there'll be a rousing overture that takes the melody from every song to summarize and reminisce over everything that's happened, and you will finally have achieved the American dream in all its Technicolor glory. So, I know my dad isn't really gay. He just likes happy endings.

Dear Virgin America,

I like underwear. I like the things it does for me and everyone who wears it. When used properly, underwear prevents chafing, keeps things warm downstairs, and plays a vital role in public health. People have been wearing it for a long time; archaeologists have found loincloths that are seven thousand years old. It's actually a surprise when someone doesn't wear underwear— whether the surprise is pleasant or unpleasant depends on the circumstances. I imagine that you make all your employees wear underwear—or at least prefer that they wear it—because the last thing anyone wants while flying is a surprise.

Now, I think we can assume that most people own more than one pair of underwear. I happen to own many pairs. In fact, I run out of clean shirts and trousers long before I run out of clean drawers. Sometimes if I haven't done laundry in a while, the only things left will be a bridesmaid dress, a Mexican wrestler costume, and pairs upon pairs of clean panties. When people run out of clean underwear, they say, "Oh dear, I'd better do laundry." This is not the case with other articles of clothing. For example, no one ever says, "Oh dear, I ran out of ascots." Truth: More people wear underwear than wear ascots. I bet that if you picked ten people out of a crowd, all ten would be wearing underwear, and maybe only one would be wearing an ascot. Or even two. But definitely not more than that.

So you can imagine my concern when I boarded Virgin America flight 317 in New York City and I arrived in Los Angeles without my underwear. Where was it, you ask? That's a good question. In fact, I asked myself the same one. My luggage was lost—on Christmas, no less. Imagine if some-one lost your luggage. How would you feel? Well, I felt worse than that. You should know that Los Angeles is a nice city, but it's even nicer when you have clean skivvies. You should also know that visiting family over the holidays is more agreeable when you arrive with presents. If you don't have them, you have to tell all your relatives—including a toothy seven-year-old—sorry, I really did buy you gifts that are proportionate to my love for you. The sad look on their faces would break your heart. It would probably break other things, too.

Not having my luggage has been a hassle. First, I had to go out and buy new knickers. But in order to do that, I needed clean ones. So I was at the mercy of the laundry machine. I watched it wash and spin while I sat around in my mother's robe, with my legs crossed. Then I waited some more be-cause for some reason, laundry takes a long time. At some point I made myself a snack. Then I put my underwear in the dryer, along with my other clothes, and waited even more. At this point I made spaghetti. When my laundry was dry, I didn't have to fold it because I had to wear it, which in some ways was kind of convenient, but not as convenient as, say, having my luggage. Then I drove to the nearest mall and bought pant-ies and socks and some clothes. I griped because I couldn't wait for things to go on sale and spent more money than nec-essary. I am what you would call a budget-sensitive person. Then I had to wash my new clothes. Once my friend got sca-bies from a sweater he didn't wash before wearing. I am what you would call a scabies-sensitive person. For the past four days, I've been wearing two different outfits, hoping no one will notice. But my aunts have noticed. They see everything. For example, they saw I didn't have their Christmas gifts.

I called you several times, and you said, don't worry, people are looking for your luggage, it is our priority. I found this to be hard to believe because if my luggage were a priority, you wouldn't have lost it in the first place. You would've lovingly placed it on a bed of handmade silk pillows so it wouldn't get jostled during a cross-country flight. Then you would've delivered it to me in an armored truck driven by karate masters. You said, Thanks for your patience, but it's not our fault—we blame it on John F. Kennedy. I said, Wait, what does John F. Kennedy have to do with anything? He's been dead for a long time. Then you said, No, John F. Kennedy International Airport. "They" lose bags fairly often—it happens. Of course, it doesn't really happen because buildings can't lose bags. This is because they don't have hands or wear underwear. But perhaps that's a lesser point. I explained that by the time my luggage was found, it would be time for me to get on a plane and go back home, and then my suitcase would be lost again. You apologized, though I found your apology lacking warmth. Also lacking: regret, requests for forgiveness, reimbursement. I asked for a free flight, an upgrade, or some cash monies. A hug, even. You said, no; we do not guarantee your luggage will arrive at your destination with you.

Now, this is a bit confusing. I know that you guarantee that *I* will arrive at my destination. But *I* am with my luggage. So, shouldn't you also guarantee that my luggage will arrive at my destination with me? You said, No, that's not the case. So now I'm even more confused, and I have no choice but to turn to math. If you recall, the transitive property of equality states that if $a = b$ and $b = c,$ then $a = c$. In these equations, a is equal to my underwear and c is equal to Los Angeles. I wonder what Mrs. Prochazka, my geometry teacher, would think about your blatant disregard for math. She'd probably give you a C, which is not a good grade. My mother would be very, very disappointed if I brought home a C. Please note that this C is different from the *c* in the equations above. You're lucky you didn't grow up with me; you wouldn't have lasted long in the house of Choi. Though, maybe you would've turned out to be an A student like me. Then you wouldn't have lost my suitcase, because honors students never misplace luggage. You know who else was an honors student? John F. Kennedy.

Virgin America, you let me down. You let math down. Where is my underwear? You must find them. Sweep the area. Bring in the dogs. Pay the ransom. There were an electric blue pair, a chartreuse pair, one with navy polka dots, and one that has red candy-cane stripes—you know, for the holidays. My underwear is quite festive, but there is no celebration at this time.

Sincerely,
Annie Choi

GOING STALLONE

"Don't say anything." I shook my head and held my index finger to my lips. "Just shush."

"It look a little . . . big for you." Her lips quivered ever so slightly. She stifled a giggle.

I glared at her. "Stop. This isn't funny. This is humiliating. I want *to die*." I stabbed myself in the throat with an imaginary shiv and made gurgling noises.

"Oh, Anne, what you can do? That smallest size I have." She bit her lip and scrunched up her face.

"Don't laugh." I wagged my finger at her. "Don't do it."

"What? I not laugh." She turned her head and pretended to cough a little. "Just cough." Hack, chortle, snort.

"Come on! This isn't funny. Don't make it worse."

"I say I not laugh!"

I looked at my reflection in the mirror. Voluminous white underwear billowed around my narrow hips. Elastic loosely circled each thigh and waves of fabric bunched up around my crotch. The large waistband sagged and dipped dangerously close to my butt crack. I stretched out the waistband with my thumb; there was enough room for me and a crew of my closest friends. Plus a dog. I inspected the panties more closely. There was a tiny boat embroidered on the front. It looked like a small ship lost in a sea of white cotton—the SS *Minnow* in the middle of a hurricane. Specifically, a Category 5, which was fitting since the underpants were five sizes too big.

I was wearing my mother's underwear.

"You look like . . . you wear . . . DIAPER!" She exploded. "YOU WEAR PAMPER!" She cranked her head back and let out a whoop. "THIS TOO FUNNY!"

"MOM!"

"You *goondoonghee* so SMALL!" She pointed to the cotton swelling over my backside. My ass was drowning in panties. The rest of me was drowning in my mother's throaty laughter.

"WOMAN, WILL YOU STOP?" I spun around to glare at her, which made my mother's underwear slide farther down my hips. I pulled them up quickly. I hate to say it, but my mother was right. My *goondoonghee* is very small.

"How you butt so small? Maybe it shrink in dryer."

"*Mom,* this is *your* underwear. My *goondoonghee* isn't small; yours is big!"

She stopped laughing and gave me the stink eye. "Anne . . ."

"I can't go out like this."

"Oh, you such baby with you Pamper." My mother gently wiped her tearing eyes, careful not to smear her makeup. "*Ayoo,* no one see, why you worry?"

"They're so huge. Look at this." I pulled the waistband above my belly button. How high up could they go? I inched them higher slowly. The waistband easily reached the bottom of my bra. I could probably have pulled them up over my chest but decided not to try.

"Oh my gosh! Look like reotard!"

"I do *not* look like a retard!"

"No, no, like bathing suit you wear for dance."

"STOP LAUGHING. I can't go out like this."

"But we have to see Grandma." My mother snickered. "Maybe you borrow Grandma panty. She smaller."

I scowled. "These *are* granny panties. You're not even a grandma, but you wear underwear like one."

"I never become grandma! You never marry and never give me grandkid."

"Will you stop? No one would marry anyone wearing these. They're like man repellent." I might as well have been better off wearing briefs made of mousetraps.

"But the panty is new! Come all the way from Korea to be on you *goondoonghee* today!"

My mother only wears underwear from Korea. She believes Koreans make the softest, most durable, and most affordable underwear on the planet. She thinks the American versions don't fit well ("Why so low? You bend over, you see everything! Why even wear panty?"). She has the same thoughts on panty hose, long underwear, undershirts, bras, and socks. Whenever she goes to Korea, she stocks up on everything. Her dresser is so stuffed she can barely pry open the drawers. Every time she opens a new pack of underwear, you can see the concern on her face. She is dipping into her savings. What if she runs out? Of course, she never will. If there is ever a Panty Apocalypse, my mother will be safe. Still, I understand how she feels. Good underwear is hard to find.

Underwear has been a source of anxiety for me ever since I started wearing it. When I was in elementary school, my mother quickly realized American underwear wouldn't fit my diminutive, flat Korean ass ("like little rice cake"). She had family friends and relatives bring skivvies over from Korea, a country full of flat asses. She'd hand them a neatly written list on the back of a gum wrapper with everything I needed, all in a range of sizes, since I was still growing. My drawers fit perfectly, but everything was in blinding colors and patterns: hot pink with stars and moons, neon green with deformed blobs that were supposed to be chicks and bunnies, thick stripes in the colors of various flags: France, Italy, and Jamaica. In retrospect, the flag underwear seems a bit disrespectful, but what did I know? I was in elementary school. I looked up the flags in an almanac that came with my favorite game, Where in the World Is Carmen Sandiego?

I remember one pair of panties was traffic-cone orange with the word "STOP!" written in boldfaced navy letters on the back. I wasn't exactly sure what I was stopping. I just knew that I—or rather my butt—was saying it rather emphatically. This coincided with the period in the eighties when everyone was wearing white pants. I went to school one day wearing my new white pants, feeling triumphant that I had escaped the plaid hand-me-down trousers that my mother had laid out for me that morning, even though I was in fourth grade and able to pick out my own clothes. Then Nick Garvey asked me why my underwear said "STOP!" and got all the other kids to look at my butt and laugh. Then he asked me if that's what people wear in China. I suppose I could've corrected him and explained that actually, no, that's what people wear in Korea, but Nick didn't care for geography, so what was the point? Instead, I choked back tears and a friend suggested I wrap my sweatshirt around my waist to cover my see-through pants. I did, and kept my ass parked in a chair as much as I could. When I got home, I took off my underwear and rummaged through my mother's sewing box and found the sharpest scissors. I started attacking my panties. Snip, stab, tear, rip.

"Anne! What you doing?"

"I hate my underwear! You can see it through my pants!"

"No, you can't, Anne."

"Yes you can! Everyone made fun of me." I poked the shears through my underwear.

My mother yanked the scissors out of my hand. "No! Stop!"

"STOP? STOP! THAT IS WHAT MY UNDERWEAR SAYS." I showed her the back of the underpants, which now said "TOP" due to my raging assault. "Why can't I have regular underwear? Why does all my underwear look stupid?"

"Anne, they from Korea, not stupid."

"Yes, they're stupid. They have stupid words and now everyone thinks I'm stupid like my stupid underwear."

"What kind of underwear you want then? White-kid underwear not fit you *goondoonghee*!"

I was frustrated. I spoke and wrote just as well as the white kids in my class, and I was better at math than all of them. I had read every Judy Blume book twice and could name all the marshmallow flavors in Lucky Charms. But genetically, my ass was from Korea, along with my underwear. My father had always stated proudly that our family was different, special. We were the only Koreans in our community. In fourth grade, I understood that we weren't like everyone else, and I was embarrassed about it. But if I couldn't be like everyone else, then at the very least, couldn't my underwear be like everyone else's?

"I want quiet underwear."

"Quiet?"

"The kind that doesn't say anything."

My mother rifled through my drawers and held up a pair of bright green panties. There was a little Scorpio symbol in the corner. I had another pair that was bright blue with an Aries symbol.

I happen to be a Virgo. I am critical and stubborn. My mother is also a Virgo.

"What about this? You wear this."

"It's *bright green*. I can't wear that under white pants. My pants are white."

"Then don't wear with white pants! Why you cut up you panty? Such waste! This come from Korea!"

"This sucks!"

"Anne, mouth."

"It's not a bad word. Sucks, sucks, sucks, sucks. This underwear sucks."

"Why you make everything so difficult?" My mother held up a pair of light yellow panties. "Try this."

"It's yellow. It'll look like I peed in my pants."

"This color not show through white pants. You try. I promise you."

"I wish I had normal underwear. I wish I were normal."

"You underwear very normal. But you not normal. You crazy."

In junior high, underwear was still being imported to our house. But undergarments had taken on a different trend in Korea—pastel satin with plenty of lace, rhinestones, and tiny silver charms. They looked like Little Miss Sunshine pageant dresses turned into panties. I didn't understand the underwear culture of Korea then, nor do I today. Thankfully, no one was wearing white pants anymore, and now it was all about black leggings. You could see the baubles on my drawers poke through my stirrup pants, but it didn't really matter because long, belted, puffy-paint shirts were the trend. My butt was safely hidden from view, but I knew no one else was wearing pink panties with fuzzy pigs in rhinestone collars. Pigs don't even need collars.

In seventh grade, I had an algebra teacher who'd had part

of his backside blown off during his service in the Israeli army. He always limped back and forth in front of the chalkboard and paused to pull up his sagging jeans and adjust his belt. I knew what he was going through. Finding normal underwear for me was a challenge, and I could only imagine his predicament. Mr. Berger rarely sat, but when he did, he placed his one unwounded cheek on a cushioned stool and leaned to one side. It looked uncomfortable. He was very open about his injury and didn't seem to care what the students thought, even though everyone made fun of him. Later "busting a sag" became trendy, and every guy in middle school was wearing his pants around his knees. The school passed rules against sagging pants and Mr. Berger joked that he'd get suspended. He was one of my favorite teachers.

During track practice in high school, girls would change in the locker room, flouncing around in their undergarments. I always changed in the bathroom stall so my teammates wouldn't see my flat chest and my flat ass clad in lavender panties embroidered with comic strip characters (complete with tiny pom-poms and googly eyes). Then in college, I found myself making out with a guy and having a horrible realization: My underwear was not sexy. In fact, it was disturbing, a bit surreal maybe. Like underwear made by David Lynch and Pee-Wee's Playhouse. I panicked. What do I do? He'll think I'm a total loser. He'll go home and tell all of his roommates that he made out with some girl wearing ruffled "Peanits" underwear with Charly and Lucy (don't ask me how they managed to spell "Lucy" right) and they'll all share a laugh and he'll sketch my underwear on a piece of paper just to get his point across and then that picture will wind up on his refrigerator and then he'll host a kegger and everyone will sit around with their red plastic cups laughing and spurting Bud Light from their noses. In retrospect, I'm sure this particular fellow would never have done that; he was probably really excited that he was making out with anyone in the first place. Guys aren't too particular at that age. If they see your underwear, they're pretty excited, even if you're wearing Pull-Ups. But that's not what a college girl thinks. My desire to take things further pretty much died and he ended up hobbling home, hunching over his erection.

The next day I went out and bought pricey, lacy underwear that chafed and slid down. I used safety pins to hold it up, which worked except it felt uncomfortable and putting them on in the first place was like getting a dress fitting with the tucking and pinching. I cut my water intake by half just so I wouldn't have to go to the bathroom and repin everything. I avoided soup. Ultimately this wasn't sustainable, so I threw everything out of my top drawer, took the last $40 out of my bank account, and went shopping again.

There were thousands of different styles of underwear, from low-rise V-thongs to seamless hip-hugger boy-shorts, and I tried them all. It was nearly impossible to find the right balance of comfort, price, and sexiness. Everything was just too big and would sag or slide down as I walked around the dressing room. I even tried on girls' panties, but with little success. They cut off the circulation to my brain. Then I went the opposite direction and tried on a pair of granny panties, the kind my mother and my granny prefer. Surprisingly, those fit.

I was faced with a quandary. Granny panties are comfortable (that is why grannies wear them in the first place) and they are also affordable (yet another reason why grannies wear them). The elastic kept the underwear on me and not on the floor, which was also a plus. However, granny panties are as sexy as a turnip. Plus, they bunch up, increasing the risk of a wedgie. Still, they fit. I deliberated in the dressing room. I even tried them on in ungranny colors like black and navy. A college-educated man would not be fooled: Things would get hot and heavy and he'd unbutton my pants and stop. *Hey, are those . . . granny panties? I didn't know they made them in red. Interesting. Oh, look at the time—I've got to go wash my hair.*

No, that wouldn't do. I decided to investigate the other extreme.

The thong rates high on the sexy (slightly trashy) scale but isn't cost-effective given the price you pay for the insignificant amount of material. It hurt when I flossed my teeth, so there was little chance I'd be flossing anything else. I pushed the thongs and all their variations aside and buried my face in my hands. I was almost twenty and wearing Snoopy underpants my aunt had brought back from Korea. To make matters worse, they were the same pair I had worn in high school. They were thin and threadbare and had tiny holes along the waistband because my waist had been growing. I had stopped receiving Korean underwear in college. I was out of the house and old enough to buy my own underwear, but I wasn't sure if this was a good or a bad thing.

Then one day, I discovered a pair of underwear that fit well and fit my budget. I remember the moment clearly. I was at the mall, browsing the intimates section of a department store. I came across a rack of panties made just for petite women. Suddenly, twittering birds and fairies appeared and a horse beckoned me with a shake of her silky white mane. *Welcome to happiness,* she said, *we've been waiting for you for a long, long time.*

The underwear was not sexy. In fact, they were downright boring, but I didn't care. They fit, they were quiet, there were no gaudy appliquéd butterflies. So, like my mother, I stockpiled all that I could. I even went to a different branch of the store and cleared out their stock for fear the manufacturer would discontinue the entire line. Luckily, they still make that underwear today—even releasing a few spicy colors and patterns, which, over the years, I have come to love and cherish. Still, they are hard to find, even online. I am going to avoid naming the brand and style here for fear that everyone who reads this will go out and buy up all my underwear. I just can't risk that. It took me two decades to get here. You can go find your own underwear, thank you very much.

When my skivvies were lost somewhere between JFK and LAX, a piece of me died. My underwear was the most valuable thing in my bag, worth more than the Christmas gifts or my favorite jeans. Losing a few pairs was like losing part of a record collection. Years had gone into seeking them out and buying them. Money could not replace the time spent looking for them and the pants-shitting joy of finding them on sale. My mother is probably the only person who truly understands this. When we die, we want to be buried with our underpants so we can have them in the afterlife. When archaeologists unearth our graves, they will be very confused. It will make the headlines: SCIENTISTS DISCOVER REMAINS OF TWO 21ST-CENTURY FEMALES, PANTIES. They will theorize that underwear was some kind of currency and that we must have been very powerful and wealthy. We will have our own exhibit in a museum, and the gift shop will start selling replicas of our underwear, along with the Monet *Water Lilies* umbrellas.

I glanced at the clock. We had to meet my grandmother for dinner and it was getting close to rush hour. We were running behind schedule.

"Maybe I should just wear the dirty ones again."

My mother looked mortified. "No, no, no. Only crazy people do that."

"People wear underwear over again all the time. I can turn it inside out."

"You wear dirty underwear?" My mother's jaw dropped a few more inches.

"Only one side is dirty." I assessed my options. Dirty ones that fit. Clean ones that don't. "Or I can go commando."

"What that mean? Like Sylvester Stallone?"

"It means not wearing any underwear."

"WHAT?"

"I don't have time to do laundry. We have to leave soon. Like thirty minutes ago."

"NO STALLONE!"

"What choice do I have?" I looked down at the shapeless, sagging mess barely clinging to my backside. It was as if someone had taken a bedsheet and poked two holes for my legs. "Look at me. This is ridiculous." I motioned to my clothes on the floor. "Everything's dirty. I have nothing to wear."

My mother rolled her eyes. "Hurry up! Wear something in my closet and we go." She shook her head as she walked out of the bedroom. "Sylvester Stallone," she muttered in Korean, "she must be out of her mind."

"Stallone was Rambo. Arnold Schwarzenegger was Commando, so actually—"

"*Ayoo*, Anne, hurry!"

I opened her closet and pawed quickly through her clothes, occasionally stopping to pull up my (mother's) underpants. How could I even borrow anything from her? I imagined myself wearing plaid golf capris, a plaid collared shirt, and a sweater vest with a patchwork golf cart, all too big. If it were warmer I could have just cut out the crotch of her panties and worn them as a skirt.

I picked up my jeans off the floor and took a cautious whiff. They smelled like Virgin America flight 317—like recirculated air, crying children, and a horrible Julia Roberts movie. I could smell the warm gutter breath of people falling asleep with their mouths agape. I cringed. I'd been wearing the same jeans for a week before even getting on the plane. There was a coffee stain on the front and something crusty on the back. Apparently I had sat in something, but what? I decided not to investigate further.

I pulled on my jeans and stuffed my mother's underwear into them. I realized quickly that zipping up my pants would be a challenge. I pulled and tugged, but the extra underwear added too much bulk. I lay down on the bed and used my hand to shoehorn myself into my jeans. I pulled in my stomach and tried to tug up the zipper. I groaned loudly.

"Why you nap? We have to go!" my mother barked at me in the doorway. She had her purse and car keys in hand.

"Does it look like I'm napping? I'm trying to get my pants on. It's not working. Obviously." White cotton was exploding from the top of my unbuttoned jeans. I felt an enormous wedgie and tried to wiggle my way out of it to no avail.

My mother howled. "You jean too tight!"

"They're skinny jeans, and hello, they fit fine when I'm wearing my own underwear. *Mom, this isn't funny.*" I pulled at the zipper a bit more and then gave up. "You know what? Screw this. I'm not going to Grandma's. I'm staying here and doing laundry. This sucks."

"But she want see you!"

I pulled off my jeans and threw them on the floor. "I'll just see her later."

"She busy later!"

"Well then I'll see her tomorrow. I'm not leaving the house until I do laundry or until I get my luggage, whichever comes first." I put on my mother's robe, the one she's worn since I was in elementary school. It's threadbare and a problematic shade of pink that makes everyone near it look jaundiced. "I don't even have her Christmas present anyway."

"Anne . . ."

"Look. I either wear dirty underwear, the same ones I've been wearing for two days now, or I don't go. Your choice."

My mother weighed the options; she has never been good at making decisions. It takes her fifteen minutes just to buy beef. She sorts through every single cut, compares prices, analyzes the amount of fat in each slab, and then narrows it down to a few choices. She stands there ruminating in front of the refrigerated shelves while thousands of customers reach around her to grab the closest steak and throw it in their shopping cart. When I was little, I looked for different cuts and offered up choices: Do you want the rib eye, New York strip, or top sirloin? I always thought the chuck was named after a person. Then in high school, after turning vegetarian, I smacked my gum and talked loudly about the evils of the cattle industry ("If we took all the grain we fed to our livestock, we could feed eight hundred million people, Mother").

I gathered my dirty clothes off the floor. "Well?"

"*Ayoo*, okay, I call Grandma."

I shuffled toward the laundry room and ran into my brother in the kitchen. He was eating a turkey sandwich. He chewed slowly and smirked.

"So, how does it feel to 'wear Pamper'?" He used air quotes to punctuate his smugness.

"Why can't you mind your own business?"

"You guys were yelling. If you don't want the entire world to know you're 'going Stallone,' then shut up about it."

"Hey, look, I have a gift for you." I pulled my hand from behind my back and flashed him the finger. An old joke we haven't grown tired of, even though it's been in heavy rotation for over twenty years.

"Dude, you lost at life."

"Can you just leave me alone? I need to do laundry."

"There's a load in there right now. You have to wait."

I groaned and felt my mother's underwear slide down a bit. I placed one hand on my hip to secure the waistband.

"Where the hell is your suitcase?"

"That's a good question."

"You should sue the shit out of them." He took another bite of his sandwich. "Sue them for ruining Christmas. For emotional hardship."

"No, I have to sue Mom for that."

"You want to borrow a pair of my boxers?" Mike burst into laughter, small bits of turkey flying out of his mouth. Mike has about a hundred pounds on me. If my mom's underwear were a boat, then my brother's would be an entire fleet of ships, an armada sailing to the New World to loot native lands and spread smallpox.

"Why can't this family just leave me alone?"

"You know better than that. You're never alone with us."

My mother finished up her call. "Anne, Grandma coming here. She bring her underwear."

Mike exploded in a guttural boom of laughter; it came straight from his bowels. He shook so hard his glasses slid down his nose.

"Mike, *shut up.*"

• • •

Finally, my luggage arrived. It took four days, which is how long it would've taken for me to drive to New York City and get my underwear. A deliveryman handed me my suitcase and I hugged it close to my chest. *Oh, where have you been?* My bag was scuffed and damp and misshapen. It had probably been left on a snowy tarmac in Queens, run over by planes and carts and refueling trucks. I zipped open my bag and cried silently to myself. "It's all right," I cooed to my panties, "you're safe, and you're here." It was just like a scene from one of those movies based "on a re-markable true story": A loved one reappears after being lost in the mountains, surviving only by sucking water out of tree bark and trapping ground squirrels. There are heartfelt embraces, damp tissues, and a sweeping orchestral soundtrack. And everyone re-alizes what is truly important.

Dear Camping,

Some of my happiest childhood memories have come from you. I loved lying in the tent between my parents and my brother, listening to the rhythmic chirps of crickets and watching moonlit shadows on the nylon walls. Our tent had a little skylight that you could unzip, and as I settled into my sleeping bag, I'd look up at the stars and the silhouettes of swaying trees. On every hike, I'd stop to examine plants and animals as the rest of my family waited impatiently ahead of me. I'd match fallen leaves to their trees, spot circling hawks, and spy on lizards with blue throats. I poked mushrooms with a stick because I was convinced they were sentient creatures from another dimension. I collected so many rocks that my pockets bulged and weighed down my shorts. I lovingly gathered pinecones, noting each specimen's beauty and shape, and then threw them all into the campfire because I liked hearing them hiss, crackle, and pop. I enjoyed communing with the outdoors, reveling in a habitat that didn't have a piano I had to practice on.

I loved you, camping, until I didn't. Now I understand what you really are: an invitation for nature to kill me. Just looking at a tree makes me sneeze. After a day in the bush, my eyes are burning, watering, and red, compelling everyone around me to ask, "Oh shit, are you okay?" It is obvious that I'm not okay. My eyes are dying. They want nothing more than to leave my blotchy, swollen face. I start hacking up my left lung, and then my right one. Then I hack something else up that looks suspiciously like my spleen. The mucus in my nose gets so thick that it seals off oxygen, and I'm forced to breathe out of my mouth, just like the close-talker at my last job. This poses a problem: Closing my mouth would mean I suffocate, but leaving it open welcomes gnats. I'm vegetarian. Either way, I can't enjoy the fresh mountain air that detergents try to imitate. Just the way watermelon candy will never taste like watermelon, a bottle of Tide will never smell like fresh air.

A hike, no matter how short, means countless bug bites that I scratch until they swell up into angry, infected boils of pus that stay for a week and then leave behind scars. I am so irresistible to mosquitoes that they bite through my clothes. Maybe I have sweet blood or maybe they prefer Korean food, with its piquant flavors. Or maybe I just emit more carbon dioxide than normal humans, because that's apparently what attracts insects. Carbon dioxide is not something I can control—even when I die I'll keep releasing it—so I have no choice but to contract West Nile, malaria, dengue fever, or Saint Louis encephalitis, all of which include symptoms like stupor and coma. But I know what you're thinking: Annie, why don't you use insect repellent? Sure, I can do that, but then I'll break out into hives because I'm sensitive to the chemicals. So then I'll take a Benadryl, which knocks me out, but not before I get emotional and tear up because life is such a beautiful mystery. I hate Benadryl.

Camping means ticks and Lyme disease, large spiders that are obviously poisonous, and insects that look like eyebrows. It also means sunburn, no matter how much sunscreen I wear, because the prescription lotion for eczema I use makes me extra sensitive to UV light. Camping involves a lot of gear: stoves, pots, pans, utensils, food, water, lanterns, sleeping bags, tents. The list goes on. We must bring an entire apartment into the wild. This means camping requires walking with heavy things. It also means cold showers or no showers and smelling like a dirty tube sock and then sleeping in a bigger dirty tube sock. You've got to stumble to an outhouse that's twenty feet away in the middle of the night, or you've got to dig a hole to do your business. Camping means poison ivy, which is nature's version of an STD.

But I love the outdoors. I really do. I understand the desire to be there and appreciate the majestic beauty of the wilderness and remember how small our modern lives are. I would just rather remember from afar—from the comfort of my own home, which is actually not comfortable at all. My apartment is about ten feet by twenty feet. This is small—think dorm room with slightly better furniture. My friend's bedroom is bigger than my entire apartment. She is six years old. The rental listing described my studio as "cozy, the perfect crash pad." It is, in fact, a perfect crash pad because it's 60 percent bed. The rest is 20 percent desk and 20 percent other (dresser, toilet). I do not have a couch. I have exactly two places to sit: right here and right there. Sometimes my apartment has no hot water. Sometimes it has no heat. Often this is in winter. Other times, the fuse blows when I use the microwave or the toaster, or if people in the building use their microwaves or toasters. I stand in the darkness with a piece of raw toast, which is the same thing as bread, and I wait for the power to come back on and the power to carry on. Sometimes this can take a day. I share my space with insects and vermin that buzz around my face or scurry across my dingy gray linoleum floors. Last month I found a half-eaten roach; I do not know what ate the other half. It certainly wasn't me. Once, after a pipe broke, it rained inside my apartment. Once, after a shelf broke, it rained books. My neighbor listens to a lot of Coldplay. I am essentially "roughing it" every day in this place. Some days are rougher than others, like today, for example. There's asbestos abatement going on in my building. My landlord promises me it is totally safe, as long as I keep my windows closed and locked—for a tighter seal—and don't run the air conditioner for three weeks. In the summer. At this very minute, my apartment is a sweat lodge. I can now carry out all my purifying rituals and make offerings to the spirit world.

Camping, please understand I've gotten soft. Squishy. Gooey. I've lost my edge; my corners are now rounded smooth. This is not your fault. Gone is my will to visit a place that's even more uncomfortable than my apartment. I don't want to sleep inside a tent, with just a thin sheet of fabric separating me from the elements. I have no desire to hike to fetch a bucket of water or worry about animals eating my food, which I do in my apartment anyway. I do not wish to sleep on rocks and twigs. If I'm going on vacation, I want to sleep in a bed, one so big that I can lie at a forty-five-degree angle with my arms and legs stretched out like a starfish. I want thick Egyptian-cotton sheets with a fifteen hundred thread count, and whenever I roll over, I want them to twirl around my legs like spaghetti on a fork. Then I want to wake up and eat spaghetti, which will be easy because I'll wake up at two o'clock, when the lunch rush is over. I want a climate-controlled, pest-free, hypoallergenic environment with a shower so strong it'll power-wash ten years of New York City grime out of my hair. I want to eat an absurd dessert that people will say I can't finish and I will prove them wrong because I am a winner. I want to breathe easy.

So, camping, I'm sorry. I'm sorry I've let you down. I've

let myself down. The mountains and forests I loved when I was ten years old no longer beckon me. Rocks and pinecones don't hold the same appeal. I am not tough enough. But you are welcome in my apartment anytime. You'll have to sleep on the floor though.

Your friend,
Annie

ROAD RASH

My father opened an atlas and slid it across the table.

"Where we live?"

I shot my hand up.

"This isn't school, dummy."

My father glared at my brother. "Mike."

"She doesn't have to raise her hand."

I dropped my hand.

"Let Annie raise her hand."

I raised my hand.

My father called on me. "Annie, where do we live?"

"Newbury Park!"

"Right, now find on map."

Mike scoffed. "Dad, she's not going to find it."

"Let her try."

I looked. It was a mysterious, overwhelming network of lines and symbols, no doubt left behind by an ancient civilization of sun worshippers. What did they mean? No one will ever know.

"Dad, she won't find it because it's *not* on the map. This is the map of the *entire United States*. Newbury Park is too small." My brother grabbed the atlas. He flipped a few pages. "Here. Where do we live, Annie?"

I looked. I shrugged.

"You can't find it? Are you learning anything in school?"

"Mike."

"What? She's in second grade—"

"I'm going to start third grade!"

"When I was in second grade I could find Newbury Park on a map." Mike was starting middle school, so he was a cartographer.

"Here?" I pointed.

"No." My brother shook his head, appalled. "That's *Northern* California. We live in *Southern* California. Don't you know north and south?"

"Yes. North is up." I pointed to the ceiling.

Mike groaned. "I give up. This is stupid." He looked at our father. "What? I didn't say *she* was stupid. I said *this* was stupid."

I raised my hand again.

"Stop raising your hand."

My father called on me again.

"Can I have a hint?"

He considered it. "No."

"Then she's never going to find it, Dad." Mike pointed to a patch on the map. "Look around here."

"I said no hint, Mike!"

"I found it!"

"Good." Our father turned to a different page and pointed to a green patch. "This is Yellowstone National Park." He put his finger on what I imagine was supposed to be Newbury Park and traced a line to the green patch. "We go from here to here. You, Mike, Daddy, Mommy, and Grandma."

"Okay. Can I watch TV now?"

"You not excited, Annie? We see Grand Canyon." He pointed to a spot on the map. "Then we see Bryce Canyon." He took a minute to look for it.

"It's right here, Dad." Mike snorted. "It's in Utah, not Arizona."

"We go Zion Canyon and Death Valley, too. We go camping in Yellowstone! You like camping!"

"Now can I watch TV?"

"Dad, you have to show her or else she won't get it." Mike left the table and came back with a volume of the *World Book Encyclopedia*, which our mother bought from a door-to-door salesman, despite her distrust of people who came to our door without a pizza. The pitch was simple: "Do you care about the education of your children?" Then our mother wrote a check. When our father found out, he got angry—not because she cared about our education, but because he thought he could've found a better price. After all, education should be affordable. But it turned out to be a good investment; my brother would pick a volume at random and read it almost from cover to cover. In fifth grade, Mike became interested in wars—World Wars I and II, Vietnam, the Seminole Wars, etc. He'd browse the photos and create detailed drawings of tanks ("The M4 Sherman actually had a flamethrower!").

Mike thumbed through the encyclopedia. "See? We're going here. It's the largest canyon in the world." He stopped and read a little. "I meant it's the largest canyon *in North America*. Do you know where North America is?"

I scowled. "Yes."

"Did you know Mars has canyons, too? Mars is *north*." Mike pointed up and smirked.

"We drive." My father smiled. "We see America!"

"But we see America every day." I looked at the pictures. The Grand Canyon looked fun, maybe. "How long will it take?"

"Two week."

"Two weeks!" I wailed. "Why can't we fly?"

"Because driving fun, Annie."

"But I don't get to drive."

"Big summer vacation! You remember for rest of you life!"

"Can I watch TV *now*?"

A few weeks later, under a blistering and unmerciful August sun, we packed up the station wagon and tied our gear to the roof. It was an old beater with six figures on the odometer and fake wood paneling inside and out. At one point, someone at Ford designed a car that matched his basement. Then he became very rich. Our station wagon was nothing but roomy. There was a bench seat in the front, a bench seat in the middle, and the floor in the back actually opened up to reveal two more bench seats that faced each other. You could seat ten, either comfortably or uncomfortably. My apartment today can't even seat three. Mike and I spread out in the back, and our grandmother and a gargantuan ice chest took over the middle bench. The cooler was stuffed with three kinds of kimchi, garlicky bellflower roots, seasoned anchovies, and dried cuttlefish. You know, typical road-trip food. My grandmother had also brought a stack of pots and pans, mixing bowls, spatulas and spoons, a variety of knives, two cutting boards, a full set of matching dishes, a strainer, a mandoline, and a bamboo sushi-rolling mat. She also brought a quart of soy sauce and a Big Gulp of sesame oil—she literally used a Big Gulp cup. There was also a ten-pound bag of rice and a rice cooker, because there are plenty of electrical outlets in the Grand Canyon to plug in one. My grandmother basically brought our entire kitchen to go camping.

We were embarking on the Great American Road Trip, something my parents had read about in books or seen in the movies when they were growing up in Seoul. Nearly all of our vacations were spent in Korea visiting family, so this was our first real big trip in the States, even though Mike and I were born here. My father was excited; he spent weeks mulling over routes and marking up maps. He never took road trips as a kid—at least not like this. South Korea is about the size of Kentucky, only with less derby. Driving across it isn't quite an undertaking. We were going to get our kicks on Route 66, or at the very least, the 101.

My father put on his seat belt and stuck the key in the ignition. "Now we go! Everyone ready?"

"No, I'm thirsty."

"You can wait, Annie." My father pulled out of the driveway.

"Here, I have water." Mike offered me his canteen, which he'd insisted on getting from the army surplus store. He wanted authentic, rugged, field-tested equipment, not the "poseur crap" from Sport Chalet. My mother was hesitant at first—military-issued gear seemed overkill for a trip spent mostly inside a station wagon. But then she discovered the prices were quite reasonable. She did draw the line when Mike wanted an inactive grenade. ("What you do with that? It not even work!")

I took a sip. "It tastes like metal."

"It's *supposed* to. It's a canteen."

Our father merged onto the freeway and settled into his seat. We were off. Kind of. We were stuck in traffic. But we were on a thrilling voyage nonetheless, one that would span thousands of miles and hundreds of hours.

For a while, I entertained myself by looking out the window, watching the landscape morph into different shapes and colors. Eventually, the eight-lane highway that weaved in and around cities turned into an endless two-lane stretch. Skyscrapers, strip malls, and tract housing dissolved into flat, open farmland. Sprinklers showered neat rows of vegetables, and rainbows bounced over heads of lettuce. Or maybe it was broccoli. My mother and her mother discussed. Spinach, perhaps? Could be cabbage—not the kind for kimchi, but the kind white people eat. This led to the topic of cooking, specifically my aunts' cooking and their fear of flavor.

I made sure everyone in the car knew when I saw a cow. I was equally impressed with horses. "Mike, is that the kind of cow we eat or the kind that gives us milk?"

Mike shrugged. "Both."

"Farmer hard work, Annie." My father looked at me through the rearview mirror. "You want to be farmer?"

"Of course she doesn't," my mother said to him in Korean, "she's going to be a doctor."

"I'm kidding." He laughed.

"I want to be a veterinarian."

My father stopped laughing. "What?"

My mother recoiled. "Oh my gosh." She translated for her mother, who spoke only three words of English, two of them being "thank you."

My grandmother winced.

Mike nudged me. "I thought I told you to never, ever say that to them."

"Why would animal need doctor?" my father sputtered. "They take care of each other."

"But sometimes they get sick."

Mike hissed, "Cut it out, Annie."

"Who go to med school just to be . . . doctor for animal?" My mother bristled.

"Veterinarians do."

Mike put on his Walkman.

"Mike, you be doctor for people, right? Mike?"

A few hours and a bag of shrimp chips later, the green rows of crops faded away and the landscape turned desolate, except for a bunch of rocks and the occasional lonesome bush. A vast nothing surrounded our station wagon and the highway in front of us snaked endlessly through a sea of dirt. The road weaved around giant slabs of rock and gently rose up and down hills. The white sky loomed large, like it was swallowing our entire car. The late-afternoon sun was beating through the back window and our air conditioner was barely conditioning.

"We in Moe Jafe Desert!" Our father grinned.

Mike snorted. "It's pronounced *mo-hah-vee*. It's a Native American word."

"I think Moe Jafe better. Look! So beautiful."

I looked. There was nothing to see. "It's hot."

"It's a desert, it's supposed to be hot." The words "you idiot" can easily be added after everything Mike says.

"Mom, turn up the air conditioner."

"It up, Anne."

"This part is Death Valley, Annie." Our father smiled proudly, as if he'd scorched this piece of land with his own hands. "Hottest place in world!"

Mike coughed. "No, it's *not* the hottest place. The Sahara's hotter." He looked at me. "That's in Africa."

I nodded. "I know."

"Do you?" He looked suspicious.

"Death Valley lowest place in the world!"

Mike coughed again. "Actually, no it's *not*, but it's lower than sea level."

"We're below the ocean?" My eyes widened. "Like, underneath it?" I was amazed and confused and shocked. It was the same feeling I had when I'd caught a lizard and it squirmed out of my hands by shedding its tail. I was left standing in our backyard with a strand of reptile between my fingers and a lot of questions.

Mike pointed out the window, at the desert. "Do you really think we're under the ocean?" (You idiot.) He grabbed a pencil and scribbled something in a sketchbook, which he had gotten just for the trip. It was already filled with planes dropping missiles on jeeps and tanks firing at jeeps. My brother did not care for jeeps—they were much too vulnerable in war zones. "It's like this."

"Got it? Good." Mike waved me off and turned to his book, a survival guide he had picked up at the surplus store. If one of us needed an emergency tracheotomy, then Mike could come to the rescue.

"You remember this, Annie." My father was enraptured by the emptiness around us. There are no deserts in Korea. "You remember it for rest of you life! Once in a lifetime!"

I had brought a pile of books, crayons and markers, a stuffed-animal panda, and a travel version of Battleship, which my brother had no interest in playing. He thought it was "interesting" that none of his torpedoes ever hit anything on my side of the board. I had also brought my Hello Kitty tea set, which Mike was even less interested in, despite the fact that there's no better time for a tea party than an endless drive through the hottest and lowest place in North America. I opened a book and began coloring. Then I stopped and closed my eyes. I felt my head spin. Air had ceased moving to the back of the car. I found it difficult to breathe.

"I don't feel good."

My grandmother woke up from her nap, sensing a grandchild was in trouble. She turned around in her seat. "You hungry?" she asked in Korean. That's the typical response in our family. If you don't feel good, it's because you're hungry. She rummaged in a bag and brought out some dried squid. *"Ojingo?"*

"No. I'm not hungry," I replied in Korean.

"Sahtang?" She held up a bag of Sunkist Fruit Gems—soft, gelatinous discs coated in sugar. They taste like partially digested gummy bears dipped in sand. They're her favorite.

I declined politely.

My mother didn't look up from her book. "Anne, just play."

My grandmother felt my cheeks. "She feels fine," she announced. She shrugged. She'd done all she could do. "You'll feel better if you draw me something pretty."

I picked up a crayon and looked at my coloring book. "I feel dizzy." I tipped my head back. I felt like I was suffocating.

Mike looked at me, alarmed. He scooted away from me. "Mom, I think she's gonna ralph."

"Who Ralph?"

"No, she's going to boot." Mike groaned. "You know, barf, vomit, hurl, upchuck, toss her cookies, do the Technicolor yawn . . . she's going to throw up." (You idiot.)

"Annie, you carsick?" My mother spun around in her seat. She had a look of terror on her face, a look I didn't see often. I did see it when Mike re-created the knife trick from *Aliens*. He stabbed back and forth between my fingers and stopped a little after our mother screamed. ("What? It's a butter knife.")

"*Mool?*" My grandmother offered me a thermos of water. She moved her head to the side so she could dodge any chum of cuttlefish and shrimp chips rising from my stomach.

Mike scooted away from me some more. I was a pariah, just like that kid in class who had lice. "Put your head between your knees so you don't puke."

My mother turned to my father. "Maybe you should get to a gas station," she advised him in Korean.

My father looked for signs along the highway. He panicked. "Annie, next one in twenty mile. Can you wait?"

I closed my eyes. "Okay."

"Hurry, Dad." Mike scooted farther away from me. "She's gonna blow." He cowered in the corner of the station wagon. "Mom, do we have a bucket for Annie's barf?"

"*Ayoo*, why we have bucket in car?" She passed back a small Styrofoam cup.

Mike raised an eyebrow. "She's going to throw up more than that."

My head spun. "I'm not going to barf."

"Nineteen more mile!" my father announced.

"If you need to barf, I can roll down the window." Mike had his finger ready on the rear-window button.

"Eighteen mile!"

My mother glared at my father. "You don't have to count down the miles," she said in Korean.

"Seventeen and half mile!"

Finally, we arrived at a rest stop. It wasn't exactly an oasis. The gas station was a bit run-down, the signs faded. There was a pile of tires and a car with mismatched doors parked to the side. My father pulled up to one of the few pumps, and I eased out of the car. The heat of the desert was overwhelming. "It's like being on the sun," I wailed. My tears evaporated instantaneously.

"You know you can't stand on the surface of the sun, right?"

"Shut up, Mike."

"Are you okay?" My grandmother gave me a long hug. It was like wearing a human jacket in the middle of the desert. I wriggled out of her arms.

My mother went into the mini-mart and came back with Popsicles for all of us. "I never see you carsick." She handed me one, which was melting rapidly. It was more like red juice on a stick. "Here. Maybe you too hot."

"I can get her some Dramamine," my brother said. "It's what pilots use in the air force."

"Why pilot get carsick?"

"No, Mom, it's for when they fly."

"Why they get sick when they fly? They pilot!"

Mike demanded money and escaped into the mini-mart. He

emerged with a Coke for himself and motion-sickness pills for me. He stuck one in front of my face. "Take it."

"Is it chewable?"

"No."

"Can you get me chewable?"

He considered it. "No."

Half an hour later, I was in the car, passed out. When I came to, I was in a bed and my mother was urging me to brush my teeth and get into the car. I didn't remember arriving at a motel. Nor did I remember eating a box of McNuggets, which I had apparently done with great McEnthusiasm. Nor did I remember getting into my pajamas. I was on a heavy trip all night, roofied by my own family.

My father buckled his seat belt. "Now we go Grand Canyon. Very big day! Annie, you remember you see in book?"

"Yes." I yawned. My head felt stuffy, yet everything was loud. This was my first hangover, at the tender age of eight.

"It very big, Annie! You should be excited! America land-mark!"

"Shhh . . . inside voice, Dad." The insides of my ears hurt, like something was clawing to get out. My brain probably.

My mother laughed. "Listen to you daughter."

"But it's *not* the biggest canyon in the world," Mike reminded us.

"Where's the biggest?" My mouth was dry. I sucked down a juice box.

"China."

"I thought they had the biggest wall."

"They have that too. They have a lot of things. Like people."

The sun clung to the sky, burning everything underneath, including me. I began scratching the crooks of my arms furiously, digging my fingernails into the delicate flesh. Tiny beads of blood formed, which I smeared away, forming a sticky red film. I'd had heat rashes since I was born, and dermatologist after dermatologist explained that I'd eventually grow out of it (which I never did).

"Stop scratching. It's annoying." Mike poked me. "Your arms are going to get infected. Then they'll get gangrene and we'll have to amputate." Which he could easily do, thanks to his Swiss Army knife and first aid kit.

Our mother passed back a tube of ointment. "Mike, put it on Anne."

"She can do it herself." Mike opened the tube for me. "Here. I don't want to touch that. It looks like smallpox."

Our grandmother fanned herself with her hand. "I'm hot," she declared.

"Me too. Make it cooler, Dad," I ordered.

My father fiddled with the air conditioner. "It high as it go, Annie."

My mother put her hand in front of the vents. "It come out warmer than before."

Mike snorted. "What do you expect? It's probably one hundred and twelve degrees outside."

"But it's two hundred degrees in here."

"No, it's not. You'd be dead at that temperature."

"The engine work very hard." Our father looked at the dials on the dashboard. "I worry we overheat."

"Maybe we turn down air con." Our mother twisted the knob.

I moaned, "No, no, no."

"Anne, we turn back up when engine cool down." She turned to my father. "This car is so old," she said in Korean. "I thought you had it all checked out before we left."

"Of course I did." He aimed the vents toward the back of the car. "I got an oil change, new tires, brake check. Everything."

"Will we make it?" My mother sounded suspicious.

"*Of course* we'll make it."

An hour later our station wagon was parked on the side of the road, hood up, engine steaming.

"Engine overheat."

"Yeah, you think?" Mike adjusted the chin strap of his boonie hat, the kind soldiers wore in the jungles of Vietnam.

Our father frowned and wiped the sweat off his forehead. "I need water."

Mike dutifully passed his canteen and our father emptied it into the radiator.

I couldn't decide if it was better to sit inside the car, where it was stifling but shaded, or stand outside, where there was a hint of moving air but also a blazing fireball. I opted to sit in the front seat with the door open, scraping my arms with my fingernails.

My father took a drag off his Marlboro. "Big mess."

My mother used a map to shade the sun from her eyes. "Why are you smoking in the middle of a desert? Aren't you hot enough?"

We flagged down some help and an hour or two later, a mechanic was looking at the engine. We needed a new part, which the mechanic didn't have. He ordered it, but it wouldn't get there for another day. Or two.

"*Ayoo . . . ,*" my mother groaned. Which is exactly what my father said after he found out how much it'd cost to fix the car. Our Great American Road Trip was turning into the Less Great American Road Trip with a Costly Delay on the Surface of the Sun, Which, Yes, Mike, We Know We Can't Stand On.

"It's highway robbery." Mike shook his head at the injustice of it all. "Real highway robbery."

The mechanic graciously dropped us off at the nearest motel. We checked into our room, and I blasted the air conditioning. I flung myself on the bed, exhausted. It's curious that sitting in a car and being bored for hours can make you tired. My mother looked around the room slowly.

"Anne, don't lay on bed."

"But it's a bed. You're supposed to lay on it."

"Get up." My mother shooed me off and gingerly peeled the blanket off the bed. She inspected the sheets and gasped. "Look, all this hair."

"Maybe it's mine."

"It's yellow hair, Annie. I think they not clean room."

"This is like that motel in *Psycho*." Mike grinned evilly. "Be careful, Annie, someone might stab you in the shower."

"*Mom!*"

"Mike, why you give her torture?" Our mother pulled off the blanket on the second bed and cringed. "Leave her alone. And ask for new room."

"Why do I have to do it?"

"Why you ask question? Listen to you mommy."

"This room is clean."

"Is this clean?" She pointed to a cigarette burn in the sheets.

We switched rooms and our grandmother got busy preparing a meal. She rinsed rice in the bathtub and plugged in the rice cooker. She set her chopping board on the desk and began dicing vegetables. Onions and garlic flew onto the carpet. She got out several pots and pans and turned on the camping stove.

"She shouldn't be using that indoors." Mike raised his eyebrows.

"Why not?" I watched my grandmother peel carrots onto a newspaper. Her hands were moving so fast I only saw an orange blur and a flash of her ring.

"The directions say to use it in a well-ventilated area. That means outside. It gives off carbon monoxide."

"What's that?"

"It's the silent killer. Duh. It's how Sylvia Plath died."

"Did she go to school with you?"

Mike pushed past me and opened all the windows, even though the air conditioner was on, rattling and humming at full strength. A gust of hot air blew into the room, which was already heating up from the stove. "I bet you the smell of Korean food's going to scare everyone in this motel."

"This motel scare Mommy." She looked around the room nervously, spying the peeling wallpaper. "Anne, keep you shoe on. I think they don't have vacuum."

The part for our station wagon didn't arrive the next day, so we had to spend another night at the motel. I rather enjoyed the subzero A/C and the three and a half channels of television. One of which was *en español*.

My father was agitated. He sat on the bed with a map spread out in front of him, rerouting our trip. He talked to my mother in Korean. "We lost two days. What should we do? Maybe we shouldn't go to Zion Canyon?"

"It'd be a shame to come all this way and not see it." My mother pursed her lips.

"But I can't take more time off from work. Maybe we shouldn't go to Bryce Canyon?"

"No." My mother shook her head firmly. "We have to see it all."

When it comes to sightseeing, my mother is like a two-year-old freebasing Fun Dip and fudge brownies on Christmas morning. She's a maniac. She'll cram everything a city or country has to offer into a single day. She'll blow through a museum, eat, shop, look at a church, look at a park, look at some monuments honoring a dead guy, eat a pastry, and power-walk across another museum all in one afternoon. This frees up the evening to see an opera.

"We can always go to Utah another time."

"We will never, ever do that." My mother refuses to visit the same place twice. She believes it's a waste of time—the world is so big; why see the same stuff over again? Last year on a trip to Rome, she rued a daylong layover in London because she had already been there before. In the seventies. "We'll just have to fit it all in."

As soon as the wagon was fixed the following day, we loaded up and took our seats. We were finally on our way again. My mother grabbed something off the dashboard and gasped.

"Oh no. This so terrible."

She held up a melted cassette. The sides were warped into a misshapen, wavy mess. If Salvador Dalí listened to cassettes, it would have been this one. Well, not this exact one. I don't think he would've enjoyed Korean folk music, which sounds like a litter of kittens in a vise. Actually, maybe he would have.

"We can listen to Weird Al!" I said. My favorite song was "Another One Rides the Bus." I hadn't even heard of Queen. I just really liked that song and, in addition, buses.

My mother cringed. "No more. Once enough."

"*Now* we go Grand Canyon!" My father adjusted the mirrors.

"Knock on wood." Mike rapped his knuckles on the station wagon.

"It's hot." Five minutes in the car and I was already scratching my arms. Mike rummaged in his (military-issue) rucksack and handed me the tube of ointment.

"We have to put air conditioner on low so car not overheat, okay?"

"But, Dad, the car will overheat on the inside."

"Then we turn up when road is flat. When we go up hill, we turn down, okay?"

I considered it. "No."

"You have no choice."

The highway to the Grand Canyon had gentle hills, and every time we approached one—no matter how small—my father would announce that he was turning down the air conditioner and then I would announce that I was hot. And dizzy. And thirsty. And queasy. And bored. My father and I went back and forth like this until Mike handed me a pill.

"Dramamine. Now."

"Mike, maybe give half?"

"Mom, she'll be okay."

"But it makes her so sleepy. Then she get so tire next day."

"But it'll shut her up."

"Mike. Mouth. Give her half."

"Okay, fine." Mike broke the pill and handed me his canteen. "Take this. You'll feel better."

"I don't want your water, it tastes like blood."

"It's iron, and it's good for you."

Soon, I drifted off, a stream of drool flowing from the corner of my mouth onto my stuffed panda.

"Wake up."

"No. I want to sleep more."

"You can't, dummy. We're at the Grand Canyon."

"Leave me in the car." I turned over on my side.

"Mom, get her up."

"Anne."

"I'm sleepy."

My grandmother reached over and stroked my hair. "Come on," she cooed in Korean, "you might like this."

I grudgingly climbed out of the car and immediately regretted it. "I think I'm catching on fire."

We walked through the parking lot, and I looked over all the license plates. Cars had come from everywhere, including exotic places like Montana and Ohio. We made our way to the lookout area, which was crowded with dozens of other people.

My father gasped. "Wow . . . look, Annie."

For the first—and perhaps only—time, our family was quiet. The canyon expanded endlessly in all directions, beyond our vision. It was impossible to see it all, to take it all in. The cliffs were striped in shades of brown, orange, and red. Rocky peaks looked like jagged teeth gnashing at the air. Ridges rose and fell steeply around the canyon and cast shadows at exaggerated angles, making parts seem menacing. Entire areas had been worn smooth by wind and water, while others remained serrated and coarse. I wanted to run my hand across the whole thing, feeling all its textures and edges. I'd probably cut a finger, but it'd be okay because Mike had plenty of gauze in his first aid kit.

"Can you believe it?" My father looked at me and smiled. "You remember this for rest of you life. Once in a lifetime!"

"Everybody, smile!" Our mother snapped a photo. "*Ayoo*, Mike, how come you never smile?"

"It's not distinguished."

I had read stories about how Paul Bunyan dragged his ax and formed the Grand Canyon. Now I imagined how Paul might have used the Grand Canyon as his living room. A rocky spire looked like the perfect place to hang a coat and the stepped walls looked like bookshelves. The mesas and massive flat-topped rocks looked like tables and stools. I could see Paul lounging in the ravine with a book. *Nancy Drew* probably.

My father sighed. "Very special, Annie." He put his hands on his hips and looked out proudly. "This only in America."

"But Mike said there's one in China."

My grandmother took in the view and smiled in approval. She had immigrated to the States only a few years earlier. Korea had mountains, rivers, plains, and coasts, just like America. But there wasn't a canyon made by a giant lumberjack and his blue ox.

Mike brought out his binoculars (from the surplus store, and "not the weak kind people use at the opera") and let everyone have a turn with them. I could make out a glistening Colorado River winding its way across the canyon floor.

Mike looked through a guidebook about the Grand Canyon. "We can hike to the bottom. We can ride asses." He saw our mother scowl. "No, I mean *asses* as in *mules*."

"I like asses." I giggled.

Our mother changed a roll of film in the camera. "No time for hike. No mule."

Mike groaned. "But we made it here. We have to hike to the bottom. Maybe go rafting."

I clapped my hands. "Let's go rafting! I want a mule!"

"Look at you grandma. She can't go raft or go mule."

Our grandmother nodded and smiled hesitantly. She may not understand English, but she can sense when people are talking about her. She and my mother exchanged words. From what I could understand, my grandmother thought we should go ahead without her and said, "I'm too old for mules."

"We should do it! Why else would we come to the Grand

Canyon?" Mike, the voice of reason. "To just look at it? Then we could've just gone to the library." Mike, the voice of a prick.

"No time. We have to go." Our mother put the camera back around her neck.

"Now? We just got here!" I tugged on our father's shirt. "What do you think?"

"I think hike is good—"

"All right then. Let's go!"

"But if we want see everything, we can't." He looked disappointed. I could tell he wanted to ride an ass. It was what you were supposed to do, part of the Grand Canyon experience.

Mike threw up his hands. "This sucks."

"Dad, you said we'd remember this for the rest of our life. We'd remember it better if we hiked to the bottom."

"Mommy and Daddy sorry." Our mother shrugged. "Blame station wagon."

"We hike at Yellowstone." Our father tried to sound upbeat.

We got back in the car and pulled out of the parking lot, swerving around the tour buses and RVs. It had taken us over three days to get to the Grand Canyon. We were there for twenty minutes.

We spent fifteen minutes at Bryce Canyon. There were spires, some rocks, dirt. We took pictures.

We went to Zion Canyon too, but I don't remember what it looks like. I'm assuming it looked like a canyon, though maybe not a grand one.

Then we began our journey toward Yellowstone. My father drove quickly through the night, barely making any stops. We were supposed to see America. Instead, we drove past it. Eventually, the landscape changed from toasted desert to golden fields, and for two days it was nothing but flat farmland heavy with the scent of manure.

"Potato," my mother announced.

"We're in Idaho. That's all they have." Mike shrugged.

"What's the capital?" I asked.

My brother looked disappointed in me. "You should know that, Annie. It's Boise."

"What's the capital of Wyoming?"

"Cheyenne."

"What about Arizona?"

"Phoenix. Why don't you just read the atlas? Or pay attention in school."

"Listen to you brother." Our mother sounded smug.

"I do pay attention, I'm just testing you. What's the capital of South Dakota?"

"Who know capital of South Dakota?" My mother clapped her hands and laughed.

Mike was not amused. "Pierre."

Along the way, we stopped briefly for gas, snacks, and my Dramamine. Mike enjoyed Ruffles potato chips, with the ridges that maximized surface area for sour cream and onion flavor, and I preferred Cheetos, Doritos, Cheez-Its, and just about anything bright orange. My grandmother, who had exhausted her supply of dried cuttlefish, settled for beef jerky, and somewhere between Idaho and Wyoming, my parents began their love affair with Corn Nuts ("So crunch!"). I hated them at the time, but now I enjoy them—especially on road trips. It's like eating your own teeth, but in a pleasant way.

We arrived at Yellowstone during the late afternoon, with the sun hovering above the mountains. I've always thought the Rocky Mountains suffer from a generic name, one that doesn't capture their rugged majesty and whatnot. Technically speaking, all mountains are rocky. It's like calling the Pacific the Wet Ocean.

"Everybody, we made it! Look!" My father smiled and pointed to a sign welcoming us to Yellowstone National Park. The sign was humble, a piece of wood with yellow painted letters. After traveling over a thousand miles, I was expecting something more impressive. Gaudy even. I wanted horns, flashing lights, stage fog, and an animatronic bear wearing moose antlers. I wanted to be welcomed with a Yellowstone theme song.

"Chuka heh yo!" my grandmother said, congratulating my father, our captain.

My mother looked back and me and Mike expectantly.

"Chuka heh yo!" we parroted dutifully.

We passed gentle rivers and streams lazily making their way across the park. Thick stands of trees would give way to lush meadows, the grasses waving and welcoming us. I wanted to ride a dappled gray steed across the knolls, my long hair flowing behind me. Or maybe skip through a patch of bright blue and purple wildflowers, occasionally stopping to stick one behind my ear. Basically, Yellowstone looked like a shampoo commercial. I wanted to wash my hair in a bucket, massaging my scalp into a thick, rich lather. I'd rinse and shake my locks out, sprinkling water all around me. Then my thick, shiny, manageable hair—now suddenly dry—would cascade over my shoulders in perfect waves, even though my hair is bone straight.

"You remember this for rest of you life!" Our father smiled at us in the rearview mirror.

"Yeah, yeah, we'll remember everything for the rest of our life," Mike mumbled.

"Once in a lifetime!"

The weather was noticeably cooler, and for the first time after a week on the road, we rolled down the windows. A warm breeze pushed the stale nacho-cheese air out of the car. I took a deep breath. It smelled like trees and leaded gasoline. It was the smell of triumph.

We made our way deeper into the park, our father driving slower than usual so we could enjoy the scenery. We passed a gold and green field with a few bobbing bodies. I slammed my fists against the window.

"LOOK! LOOK! DAD, STOP! PULL OVER! PULL OVER!"

"Okay, okay, Annie, calm down."

I scrambled out of the car, taking just enough care to not slam the door and scare away the animals. One eyed us warily and then continued eating.

"They're elk."

"I know, Mike." I rolled my eyes.

"So, you know what elk are, but you don't know the capital of Arizona?"

"I saw them on *Wild Kingdom*." I nodded proudly. "Elk aren't very smart."

"How do you know?"

"Because they're food for other animals."

The elk had sandy brown coats, with darker, shaggier fur on their thick necks and heads. They were much larger than the deer I'd seen at the L.A. Zoo. They were heavier and taller, with barrel chests and big bellies that swayed as they walked. They had long, willowy legs that looked like they could leap over anything, only to crumple upon landing. A few had small coatracks on their heads.

"They shed their antlers every year and when they first grow back, they're fuzzy!" I spouted.

Mike shrugged, unimpressed.

Our mother snapped a photo. "Wow, deer!"

"They're elk," Mike and I said in unison.

"Oh, *sorry*."

Our father grinned. "Look at all this. You remember for rest of you life."

"We know." My mother winked at me.

"Once in a lifetime!"

"We *know*."

Finally, we arrived at our campsite, deep in a network of colorful tents and less colorful RVs. I got out of the car and explored the area, a small clearing with a fire pit and a wood picnic table. I peeked behind the trees and rocks and inspected the bushes. It was early evening and the gnats and mosquitoes were swarming around my head.

"What are you doing?" Mike, duffel bags in hand, glared at me.

"I'm searching for bears." I crouched down and investigated the campsite floor for bear tracks, whatever those looked like.

"Why don't you help unload the car?"

"Because I'm searching for bears."

My mother and grandmother got busy with dinner, fermented soybean and mushroom stew, which is exactly what the pioneers ate. My grandmother walked over to the bathrooms and plugged in the rice cooker, no doubt a strange sight for the fellow campers living off of peanut butter sandwiches and grilled hot dogs. My mother opened a jar of kimchi, and the acrid, spicy smell traveled across the campsite and beyond. Somewhere animals were either excited by or scared of our food.

Meanwhile, Mike and our father began setting up the tent. Judging by the box's picture, we were about to sleep in a nylon mansion with happy white people.

"Do you think we'll see a bear?"

"No." Mike was fussing with a knot, following a diagram in his survival guide.

"How do you know?"

"Animals don't like to be seen."

"But people like to see animals."

The first night in the tent I lay awake to the sounds of crickets and rustling leaves. I listened for a snap of a twig or crunch of dirt—any sign of movement outside our taut nylon walls. I imagined late at night, after everyone had gone to sleep, elk, raccoons, porcupines, badgers, and other glassy-eyed woodland creatures would come out. They'd stroll through the campground and check out our car, which held our food. They'd whisper to each other, gossiping and chortling, like prissy ladies at tea. Then the bears would arrive. There'd be chaos and carnage. The dumb, feeble elk would succumb to the barbaric, limb-tearing fury of savage bears. It would be an epically one-sided battle. At some point, I remembered that bears ate boring stuff like berries and garbage, so the elk would actually be okay. I was disappointed. Whenever I watched *Wild Kingdom,* I always rooted for the predators—they deserved to win because they were so much cooler. A jaguar should eat whatever it pleases. Eventually my mind wandered further and I fell asleep, my family breathing heavily around me.

The next day, we had a full schedule of sightseeing and hiking, courtesy of my mother. She warned us repeatedly to wear "comfortable shoe." We began with Old Faithful.

"Do you know what geyser is, Annie? Did you learn in school?" My father pulled into a parking lot. "It erupt like volcano, but instead of lava, it has water."

"Just water?" I shrugged. "So it's a mountain that sprays water?"

"No, not mountain. Water come up from ground."

"Oh. So it's just a hole on the floor?"

"Dad, you're not explaining it right." Mike disapproved. If he could have, he would've brought the entire set of *World Book Encyclopedia*s on our trip.

There was a crowd of people around the area, and a rope prevented anyone from getting too close. I couldn't see much except steam billowing from the ground, rising up to meet the puffy clouds above. I was nominally intrigued. "Why does it smell so bad?" I scrunched up my nose.

"Hydrogen sulfide!" My father grinned. "Formula H-two-S."

"That formula for spoil egg!" My mother laughed. "You daddy so smart."

Mike translated for me. "The smell is from sulfur. That's stuff in the rocks, okay?"

I nodded.

"No, not sulfur. Hydrogen sulfide. It's gas." Our father glared at Mike. "Annie, water inside the geyser can be two hundred fifty degree Fahrenheit! Very, very hot. Do you know water boil at two hundred twelve degree Fahrenheit?"

"Yes," I lied.

"What that in degree Celsius?"

"Dad, she's not going to know that." Mike turned to me. "So you know how it gets really hot underground, like in the middle of Earth?"

"Yes," I lied.

"The water boils underground and it gets really, really hot and then it erupts and water shoots up, like a fountain except it goes high up."

"When will it erupt?"

"Soon."

"How soon?"

"You have to wait." My mother snapped a photo of us. "Be patient."

"Maybe one hour." My father looked at his watch. "It called 'Old Faithful' because we depend on it. You know what 'faithful' mean, Annie?"

"Yes," I lied.

"What he means is that it erupts on a schedule, kind of," Mike whispered. "Just ignore everything he says."

I laughed. And then waited. And waited.

And waited some more.

"How long do we have to wait? We should call it 'Old Boring.'"

"Anne." My mother looked stern. "Be nice."

"Geysers don't have feelings."

I was expecting an epic water show, with dazzling jets arching across the sky and rousing music with an eager horn section. Maybe I'd get soaked, like the time I went to SeaWorld. But when Old Faithful finally did erupt, I quickly realized it was just a hole in the ground shooting up a stream of water. It was over in a minute. No colors, no lasers, no killer whale. "That's it?"

"You didn't like?" My father was concerned. "It very special! You remember this for rest of you life. Once in a lifetime!"

"No, not once in a lifetime, Dad. It'll erupt again in ninety minutes." Mike pointed to a sign.

I shrugged. "I've seen it before."

My mother raised her eyebrows. "Where?"

"At Disneyland. When they do the pirate show."

My grandmother clapped and beamed. "Let's see it again!"

"Again?" Mike groaned.

"It's not *that* special." I groaned too.

"If you grandma want to see again, then we see again." My mother sat down on a bench as groups of tourists began leaving the area. No one else seemed impressed enough to watch it again.

Later we visited other hot springs and geysers, which were even less impressive than Old Faithful. The exception was the Morning Glory Pool, with its brilliant blues, greens, and yellows.

"It's from bacteria." Mike leafed through a pamphlet from a park ranger. "They're different colors."

"How do they live if it's boiling in there?"

"This one's special because it's not that hot."

"So can we go in it?"

"No. That'd be breaking the law. Federal law. Yellowstone's a national park." Mike shooed me and my stupid idea away.

Turns out my grandmother wanted to go in it too. She had a membership to Bally's gym just for the Jacuzzi.

"No, Grandma, we can't or else we'll go to jail." I spoke in Korean but didn't know the word for "jail," so I mimed handcuffs.

My grandmother smiled and took a deep breath, sucking in the noxious fumes. "Breathe it in, Annie. It's good for you."

I pinched my nose.

"It clears your body. Makes your skin better."

Koreans are obsessed with skin. Practically every commercial on Korean television peddles a cream, gel, ointment, unguent, or poultice that moisturizes, clarifies, and/or detoxifies skin. There are complicated skin-care systems that require a regimen of scrubs and toners, along with daily doses of magical pills that keep skin taut and blemish-free. There are even beverages and snacks designed to smooth wrinkles and fade spots. I've seen magazine ads for lotions developed by attractive but serious scientists, and salves made of fruits, vegetables, and herbs. In other words, a salad. Traditionally, fair skin is a sign of beauty and class (aristocrats stayed pasty indoors while field workers got toasted to a warm, golden brown), so there are cosmetics designed to lighten and whiten and turn you transparent. Everything is, of course, endorsed by celebrities whose flawless skin is made possible by the Photoshop stamp tool.

My chronic rashes were a source of concern, especially as scratches turned into unsightly scars. My grandmother fed me tomatoes because she thought they'd clear up my skin and keep my cheeks rosy. She also thought eating white foods would help— tofu, taro, pears. Once she returned from Seoul with special fish oil to rub on my arms, which made my rashes worse and, in addition, smelled like hot trash. Then she told me to eat the oil instead, which resulted in acrid burps that were unladylike and inhuman. Nothing helped my skin.

I let everyone know I was sick of looking at holes of hot water, but we forged ahead anyway—my mother wouldn't be satisfied until she saw every spring in the park. According to the guidebook, there were ten thousand of them. We began an easy hike through an area that, according to Mike, would be "heavy with geothermal activity." It certainly smelled that way. The midday heat was prickling my arms and I began to scratch with vigor. Even though the weather was cooler than in the desert, my rashes were still flaring up.

"Annie, no scratch." My mother cringed at the sight of my bleeding arms.

"But I'm itchy, so I have to itch."

"Mike, give her ointment."

Mike dutifully reached into his rucksack, only to come up empty. "I don't have it. Must be in the car."

My grandmother held my hand so I couldn't shred my arms. The desire to scratch was overwhelming. It's similar to the urge to pee, when it's gotten so severe it's the only thing you can think about. "Can you blow on it?" I asked her. "It'll make it feel better."

My grandmother obliged. It helped a little. Maybe. She patted my back. "We'll make you feel better." She reached into her purse and took out a flowery handkerchief. Then she slowly stepped over a low rope and went rogue, throwing caution and federal laws to the wind. She began walking up to a hot spring.

"Grandma! Where are you going?" I panicked.

My mother went after her. They talked quickly, my mother shaking her head. I could see my grandmother wave my mother away.

"Dad? What are they doing?"

My father sighed and stepped over the rope, leaving my brother and me behind.

"Come on, Mike, let's go."

Mike glanced around, looking for narcs. "Okay, we're clear. Let's go."

Everyone was gathered around a small hot spring, just big enough for a person to soak in. My grandmother gingerly stepped toward the water's edge.

"*Oh my God,* is she going *in*?"

"Anne, shhh. She not go in. She just go near it." My mother looked concerned. And maybe a little curious.

"What do you mean go *near* it? She can be *near* it from the other side of the rope." Mike pointed back to the hiking path. "We have to go back."

"What if she falls in?" My heart was pounding; I could feel it in my stomach.

"That water is over two hundred degrees!" Mike's eyes widened. "Dad! Stop her!"

"SHE'S GOING TO BOIL TO DEATH!"

My grandmother ignored all of us. She crouched down and dipped half her handkerchief in the water. She swished it around.

"What is she *doing*?" I jumped from foot to foot in a panic.

"She's breaking the law." Mike looked around nervously. "We're not allowed to be here."

I imagined my grandmother being thrown against a squad car and handcuffed. One cop would look through her purse, wary of her dried fish snacks and *hanyak*—medicinal herbs. Another cop would read her her rights, which my mother would try to translate in Korean through desperate tears. My grandmother would spend the rest of her life in jail, complaining about the white-people food. She'd befriend a con doing a five-to-seven on a B & E. I watched a lot of reruns of *Hawaii Five-0*. It was my brother's favorite show and he'd wrestle the remote away from me so he could watch it. He learned to play the theme song on his saxophone.

My grandmother gasped. "Hot! It's hot!" She balled up the handkerchief and threw it back and forth between her hands, trying to cool it down like a hot potato. A really, really hot potato. *"Ahya! Ahya!"*

"Grandma, get away from there!" I waved my arms around. I could picture her falling into the spring, her clothes bursting into flames. Her skin would melt from her body, leaving a bloody carcass that would eventually boil off until there was just her frail skeleton floating in the water.

My mother reached over and helped her up, my grandmother now swinging the handkerchief around like a flag. My brother and I stared, dumbstruck.

My grandmother offered me the handkerchief. "Here you go, Annie. It's hot, but not that bad."

"What am I supposed to do with this?" I asked in Korean. It reeked like rotten eggs.

"Put it on your arms."

"What?"

"Put it on your rashes. Go on."

"Really?" I looked up at my mother. "Is that okay?"

"No. It's not." Mike scowled.

My mother seemed conflicted. "Grandma think it help you stop itch."

"Grandma is wrong."

"Mike, shh."

"She's crazy."

"Don't call you grandma crazy."

"Mom, she almost *died* back there."

My grandmother nodded at me. "Do it. You'll feel better, I promise."

I was wary. Once when I had a stomachache, my grandmother served me *hanyak* that tasted like a fireplace. It didn't help. She also tried to cure my headache by writing on the bottom of my foot. I don't remember if it worked, but it was fun trying to see what she wrote.

"Do it before it cools down."

The handkerchief was hot but strangely soothing against my arms. It smelled like our refrigerator after a blackout.

"You feel better?"

"Maybe?"

My grandmother smiled. Success.

"The bacteria is going to give her an infection." Mike shook his head.

"She be okay." My mother inspected my arms, which were bright red from the heat, the rash, and a scalding hankie. "See? She stop scratch already."

"Who knows what kind of damage she caused to that hot spring?" Mike bent down to take a closer look at my arms. "When we get back, I'll give you Bactine and Neosporin," he whispered.

"Okay," I whispered back.

It wasn't until a few years ago that I found out sulfur is used to treat eczema and skin irritations. There's no scientific research on it, but the ancient Greeks used it.

By the time we returned to our campsite, it was dusk. After dinner, we sat around the fire, the adults chatting while Mike and I threw various things into the fire pit. My brother gathered sticks for marshmallows and taught our grandmother how to make s'mores, which she proclaimed were too sweet. She has a salt tooth.

The rest of our trip was a blur—there was some hiking, a waterfall, a picnic with wasps. I counted birds and listened for different songs. I petted mossy tree trunks like they were cats. I collected curiously shaped rocks and lined them up in front of our tent. I thought every constellation was the Big Dipper.

One morning, I woke up to a hand shaking my shoulder.

"Shhh, Annie. Get up." My father unzipped my sleeping bag. "Be quiet."

"Huh?"

"You have to see," he whispered. He shoved shoes on my feet and pulled a sweater over my head.

I yawned. "Is it time to wake up?" I looked around the tent. I could make out three slumbering mounds underneath the blankets and sleeping bags. "What about them?"

"Hurry. Go outside," my father whispered. He picked up my jacket off the floor. "You have to be quiet, okay?"

He walked me through the campsite, prodding me to move faster. I stumbled over some rocks in my sleepy haze. Twigs snapped under my shoes, which he had loosely tied in our rush.

"Where are we going? Bathroom? I don't have to go."

"You see."

It was early; there was a glow of yellow and pink on the horizon. I could see my breath. On chilly days, I liked to pretend I was smoking Marlboros, just like my father. I'd put two fingers up to my lips and try my hardest to imitate his face—a look of quiet reflection tinged with a relief that can only come from a nicotine fix. Eventually, my mother exiled him to the garage to smoke and then, later, to the sidewalk.

My father led me to a small meadow near the edge of the campgrounds. He pointed at some large shapes on the grass. "Look. Can you see?"

"Wow." I covered my mouth so I wouldn't squeal.

A group of animals was eating its way across the clearing. They were imposing, heavyset beasts with large humpbacks that sloped down to a smaller rump. Their coats were dark and shaggy around their head and neck but smooth around their haunches. Their heads were enormous and hung low to the ground, as if their necks couldn't support the weight. I could see their small, curved horns, though their eyes blended right into their woolly faces. They had bushy domes of fur on the crowns of their heads; it looked like they were wearing fuzzy caps, the kind Russian spies wore. Their legs were short and thin, and I was amazed something so dainty could support all that weight. It was like a giant, furry boulder balancing on four little sticks. They grazed in silence, their short tails whipping back and forth. I held my breath, as if the act of being alive would scare them away.

"They buffalo, Annie."

"I know."

I stood there, absorbed, taking in every movement, every detail—the flick of a tail, a twitch of a head, a sway of a beard. It was a moment my father had made just for me, to tell me, yes, Annie,

I'm listening, even when we're all arguing or complaining or dismissing your grandmother's skin treatments or your aspirations to become a "doctor for animal." We watched the herd silently until the sun finally rose. My father pleaded with me to go back to bed before my mother woke up.

Dear Department of Motor Vehicles,

Good afternoon. I want to start by saying that I know you have a very tough job. I read that there are over 250 million registered vehicles and over 208 million drivers in the United States right now. That's a lot. You must have a lot of work. I can't even imagine how much work you have. This morning I woke up and made myself coffee and it was so much work I had to take a coffee break afterward. So believe me when I say that I understand how demanding your position must be. However, this does not stop me from expressing my disappointment.

The other day, I was walking down Broadway when I saw a truck graze a double-parked van and tear off its side-view mirror. The mirror sailed a few feet into the street and shattered into a million pieces. A million! I know because I counted them. To say the least, the mirror could not be saved. Another life lost because one driver lacked spatial skills and another one had double-parked on Broadway. Broadway is a busy road. It doesn't even matter what city this Broadway was in. Broadways all over this country are broad, busy roads. Isn't there a law that states you can't double-park on a Broadway? If there isn't, there should be. I don't want to tell you how to do your job, but you should look into that.

Just yesterday, I was walking down West Broadway, which is west of regular Broadway and just as broad, and I saw half a dozen cars blocking a busy intersection. Half a dozen! That means six! Traffic was backed up for blocks because these six entitled drivers felt it was acceptable to park in an intersection. These six drivers also felt it was acceptable to lay on their horns, as if it was everyone else's fault traffic was not moving. This honking, of course, caused other drivers to honk. As if to say, "Hey! Stop honking!" Honk, honk. This caused pedestrians to yell at the honking drivers, which, in turn, caused babies to cry. The takeaway lesson here is that bad driving makes babies sad. I'd like to remind you that the children are our future.

At this very second, there are dented bumpers, blown-out tires, bits of engines, and the occasional appendage littering every highway from US 1 to US 830. There is excessive speeding, excessive slowing, excessive tailgating, and a whole lot of Bluetooth headsets that make people look like they're robots from the future—a very lame future where robots are stuck in traffic because they can't fly. Somewhere in America, there's a driver who's ignoring lane lines and road signs and swerving between cars and pedestrians while texting and eating a Taco Bell Meximelt and watching DVDs and singing along to "Life Is a Highway" all at the same time. It's not even a good song. And I bet you didn't know this: It's not by John Cougar Mellencamp.

Right now there are just too many people on the road who shouldn't be there. They are the ones who speed at one hundred miles per hour, only to get stopped at the next red light. They are the ones who bust through stale yellows, jump the reds, or stay stopped when the light changes to green because they are too busy not driving. They are the ones who park in crosswalks, take up two parking spots, or park a mile from the curb. They are the ones who turn right from the left lane, turn left from the right lane, or make U-turns despite the signs that say NO U-TURN. There are even people who can't do

U-turns. Instead, they do three-point turns in the middle of a busy boulevard. Driving requires attention, skill, knowledge of local laws and customs, common sense, and good manners. It's not for everyone. There are many things that aren't for everyone—oboes, veganism, neckbeards.

Listen, you don't have to let everyone who passes your tests drive. You really don't. Think of your organization as a club. Not like a book club or an auto club, but more like a nightclub, you know, a trendy cha-cha palace where the music is too loud, the bar is too crowded, and the drinks are overpriced and weak. The kind of place everyone wants to go to. The kind of place with a bouncer. The bouncer decides who gets in and who doesn't. There's no real reasoning behind it either. People line up for blocks, sometimes suffering in the cold, and the bouncer takes one look and says, "Hey, I like your jaunty and festive hat, you can come in," or "No way, I don't like your shoes, you stay out. Forever." The bouncer's very high and very arbitrary standards ensure that everyone inside the club has really nice shoes and accessories, which, I think we can agree, can really make an outfit. The bouncer also throws people out of the club when they misbehave; it's an important responsibility that ensures everyone's safety. Remember, "safety first." I'm pretty sure you taught me that.

So, that's what the Department of Motor Vehicles needs— a bouncer. The good news is that I'm here to help. I happen to have very high and very arbitrary standards. I'm not afraid to tell people they're not allowed to drive. In fact, I just told that to somebody this morning. I think you'll agree that this solution will restore peace and order to our streets. In addition there are some other benefits, like fewer car accidents and fewer cars on the road, which would also decrease carbon emissions. What that means is that together we can actually save our environment. So, save Earth. Think of the polar bears, the children, the future, whatever.

Let's arrange a meeting to further discuss how my skills could benefit you. You'll see how my experience—both in and out of the car—can improve humanity. I'm available next Tuesday and Wednesday. I'll be taking public transportation.

Sincerely,
Annie Choi

DRIVER'S ED

My mother looks at me. I look at my mother. It is a showdown in the LAX parking lot. I have just arrived from New York after a long flight plagued by delays, a near-miss connection, and gut-twisting turbulence. My legs are numb, my back is stiff, my neck is pinched, and my stomach doth protest too much. I am exhausted, but with just enough energy to be irritated by everything—I mean, do we *really* need signs that remind people to lock their cars? I've already got road rage and I'm not even inside a car. It's clear that I shouldn't drive, especially on the 405, arguably the nastiest freeway in America, with its "carmageddon" traffic and construction.

"Mommy can drive."

"I want to drive."

"I can do it, Anne."

"I know you can, but I can too. Let me drive."

"You look so tire. You should sleep."

"Seriously, I'm fine. I drank enough coffee for both of us." I stretch out my hand for the keys. "Hand them over." I wiggle my fingers.

"But look at you face! Very puff, like mushroom."

"You mean marshmallow."

"No, I mean mushroom, with short body and big, puff head." She laughs. I don't.

"I don't want to argue, I just got here. Please?"

"Fine, fine, but drive safe."

"I prefer to endanger our lives, if that's okay by you."

She rolls her eyes. "So sarcast." She rummages through the donkey feed bag she calls her purse and fishes out the biggest mass of crap I have ever seen in my entire life.

"Whoa, what is this?"

"Mommy car key. What else?"

There's a stretchy spiral bracelet that looks like a telephone cord, a charm picturing the Virgin Mary, a plastic tag with the contact information of an auto body shop, a silver plate with the name of her church, a little metal fork for prying golf tees out of the ground, and a large rubber head of Marvin the Martian, a cartoon character who wants to destroy Earth because it obstructs his view of Venus. There's also a stuffed animal attached to her keys. An actual stuffed animal. It's a duckling wearing a baby bib and a bonnet. It's probably the size of a real duckling. All this garbage hangs from a ring that has only two keys.

"Why do you have all this junk? It's ridiculous."

"This way I never lose."

I get in the car and stick the key in the ignition. The duckling lies across my lap, its bill pointed toward my crotch.

"How come you always want drive?"

"Because . . . I never get to drive in New York."

The truth is I don't actually like driving. I don't hate it, but I don't enjoy it either. But when I'm with my mother, I want to drive. I need to drive. It's imperative. This is because when my mother is driving, I am that much closer to death. There's still a lot I want to do with my life.

A good portion of my mother's life is spent behind the wheel, shuttling between the far edge of the Valley and Koreatown practically every day. She often slogs across Los Angeles to run errands and chauffeur her sisters, who can't/don't drive, or she heads to Orange County to golf with friends, easily a two-hour trek with traffic, each way. She takes road trips with her church group and schleps over an hour to go to a farmer's market and buy peaches. She's been known to drive across the Valley just to pick up dry cleaning and then drive all the way back. She easily burns through a tank of gas every other day; the hole in the ozone layer is shaped just like her car. Given the sheer number of hours she spends on the road, my mother hasn't had *that* many accidents. Still, she's had her fair share. Backing into things, rolling over things, making ill-timed left turns, sideswiping trucks, rear-ending cars. Given the way she drives, however, I'm surprised she doesn't crash every day.

I, on the other hand, have never had a car accident. I'm a good driver.

Now, I realize practically every driver thinks that. There are very, very few people who say, "You know, I'm a horrible driver, I can't believe they even gave me a license, I should give it back." Some people will admit to a crime, but they'll never, ever admit they're a bad driver. I actually have friends who say they drive even better when they're high or that they're great drunk drivers. (My response: "Only a drunk person would say that.")

But, really. I'm a good driver.

"Don't kill you mommy. I go church tomorrow." She double-checks her seat belt to make sure it's secure.

"There's nothing to be afraid of." I turn the key and the engine rumbles awake.

"Anne! Look behind!" She grabs my arm.

"I haven't even put the car in reverse yet."

"Okay, look behind first. Then go back."

"Be cool, woman." I make a big show of checking behind me. "I'm looking to the left. Now to the right. Now I'll look at the left one more time before backing up the car."

My mother nods. "Very good."

I pull out of the lot and onto the street.

"Anne, get in right lane."

"I will in a minute."

"No, get in right lane now because freeway on right side."

"I know, but we have a few miles."

"So much traffic later, you have to change now."

"That lane's slow. I'll change in a bit."

"I telling you, Anne. Change."

"But that side has traffic."

"Anne!"

"Okay, okay, Jesus."

"Jesus help you driving."

I look over my shoulder to see if I'm clear to change lanes. My mother does the same.

"You can change now."

"I know, Mother."

"Don't forget to turn on signal."

"It's already on, don't you hear it?"

"Someone let you in! Move over!"

"I *know*." I gun the engine and slip into the space.

"Oh my gosh!" She grabs the handle above the window, the one usually used for hanging dry cleaning. I call it the oh-shit grip. *"Do slow!"*

"I *am* going slow! We're fine. See? You're still alive and everything." I pause. "Though, I might kill you."

"Turn right for freeway. We go four-oh-five north!"

"I know how to get home." We get on the freeway and I immediately turn on the signal to change lanes.

"Why you change lanes?"

"Because I don't want to be in the slow lane. It's for slow people."

"Like Forrest Gump?"

"Sure."

She looks hurt. "Mommy always drive in this lane."

"I don't know how to respond to that." I look over my shoulder to check for cars. My mother does this too.

"Mom, you don't have to do that."

"You can change lane now. Go! Go! Hurry!"

I change lanes, and then change another. I decide to go all the way to the fast lane, so I change again.

Meanwhile, my mother is holding on to her oh-shit grip tightly. "Why you swerve?"

"Changing lanes is not the same thing as swerving."

"You go too fast!"

"I'm not going too fast." I glance at the speedometer and slow down a little. "I'm going the speed limit."

"Why you lie?"

"What are you talking about? I'm not lying. I'm *driving*."

"Police come get you."

"You make it sound like I'm a criminal. I'm a responsible member of society!" I shake my head. "I have a 401(k)!"

"Get over to right lane now."

"Why?"

"Because we go one-oh-one north."

"That's not for another ten, fifteen miles."

"Change now."

"No. The right lane has traffic. Why would I sit in traffic when I can pass it all?"

My friend Nathan is one of those aggressive drivers who aren't afraid to be a total asshole. He'll zoom down the shoulder and then cut into a long line to turn or exit. He bullies his way into the tiniest space between cars without remorse and often complains that his horn is too feeble, just like the people who ride scooters. He has repeatedly told me, "Turn signals are for the weak!" Whenever I ride with him, I always feel vaguely guilty and look apologetically at the suckers behind us. I suppose he's a good driver if you're in the car with him and a bad driver if you're not. My mother wouldn't last a minute riding in his car. Nor would he with all her backseat driving.

Soon, we merge onto the 101. Surprisingly, traffic is moving freely. I release my hand from the steering wheel to fiddle with the stereo.

"Anne. Both hands on steering wheel."

"I'm just turning on the music. It takes half a second. See? Now my hand is back on the steering wheel, and we get to listen to some hot jams. You love Usher!"

Some mothers prefer white men in tuxes crooning tired, bland standards. My mother is down with the Ush ("His voice so big and he dance like Michael Jackson!"). For her birthday, I got her an Usher CD. The cover pictured him with his shirt wide open, his sculpted abs and chest sizzling in baby oil.

My mother sings along. "'Next thing I know she on me scream, "Yeah, yeah, yeah!"'"

I wonder if she understands what she's singing. Once at karaoke I realized a song I've loved since I was ten is actually about a guy trying to tame a wanton ho and not really about a little red Corvette.

Suddenly, a look of horror washes over my mother's face. "Annie! Stop! STOP!" As we come over a gentle hill, there is a sea of red brake lights.

"What?"

"BRAKE!"

"Huh? We're fine."

"ANNIE!" She grabs my arm. "BRAKE! BRAKE NOW!"

I wave her off. "We're okay. I don't have to slam on the brakes."

"*Stop!* Slow down! You going to hit!"

"No, I'm not braking."

"YOU GOING TO KILL MOMMY!"

"I have plenty of time to come to a stop. First, I slowly release the gas pedal, but I'm not pressing on the brakes yet. I just gently let go of the gas. Very, very gently, see? It's very smooth. We're slowing down now. I've released the gas, and now I'll push on the brakes. Very gently. We're slowing, we're slowing, we're slowing down . . . now . . . we've stopped. No accidents. See? We're alive."

She scoffs and tightens the seat belt across her chest. "How you learn how to drive this way?"

"What are you talking about? I'm a good driver!"

I actually failed my learner's permit exam and had to take it again. There are a lot of arcane questions about the speed limit in a blind intersection or how much time you have to notify the DMV after you sell your car. It's an exam specifically designed to fail fifteen-and-a-half-year-olds. Eventually I passed because my friend Karen whispered a few answers from her desk. Yes, I cheated. Do I regret it? Not really. But, to be clear, this doesn't make me a bad driver, rather more like someone with a friend who actually read the driver's handbook cover to cover.

When Karen and I received our learner's permits, we danced around the DMV parking lot with our shit-eating grins. We were

officially mature enough to get behind the wheel and learn to
drive. Soon I wouldn't have to beg my mother to take me to the
mall or drive me to Alyson's house. Soon I wouldn't have to wait
for her to pick me up after track practice and yell at her for being
forty minutes late or for forgetting altogether. I was so close to
freedom, I could taste it. It tasted like late-night curly fries at Red
Robin and juicy gossip about our crushes.

But first, I had to learn how to drive.

Mike's car was passed down to me since he was away at
college—a late-eighties blue Volvo built like a tank. When my
brother bowled over a mailbox, there wasn't even a scratch. When
he backed into a truck, the bumper got the tiniest nick. (My
brother is not the best driver, or even a good one.) At one point,
the Volvo caught on fire due to a faulty oil filter and it survived.
Basically I could drive this beast through a monster truck rally
and arrive home unharmed. I actually called it the Beast, after the
X-Men character—a blue and burly yet highly refined and reliable
mutant. That was the Volvo. But while my physical well-being was
not at risk, my emotional health was in the danger zone. Who
would teach me to drive? Dad or Mom? Tough choice. The toughest I'd ever faced. Until that point it was "Should I wear my hair up
or down?" or "Can I really wear a vest with shorts?"

Even at fifteen and a half, I could appreciate my father's driving
skills. I always felt at ease when he was behind the wheel. He was,
and is, a smooth driver. So smooth, in fact, that he lulls me into a
pleasant daydream, one where I'm relaxing in a nineteenth-century
cottage in Burgundy. Riding with my mother, however, is a series
of horrifying nightmares that never ends until the gearshift is in
park. But, at fifteen and a half, I understood that my dad was long-
winded. Once he took an hour to explain how to use the answering
machine, which had complex buttons like "play" and "stop."

I knew my mother's driving was far less than exemplary. On more than one occasion, I'd yelled at her to watch for errant shopping carts and pedestrians. Taking driving lessons from her would be like taking acting lessons from William Shatner. There are just better people to learn from. However, my mother's way of doing things is to just do them. She jumps right in without hesitation. In high school she liked to hike trails for the experienced: "You see mountain and you go up." No big deal. Driving with my mother meant that I'd actually learn how to drive by actually driving, and not by listening to someone talk about driving. But there'd be a lot of yelling. A lot of it.

It was a lose-lose situation. Choose one: Eat a bowl of hairy spiders or a bowl of cockroaches. Get punched in the nose or in the mouth. Remove your left or right testicle. Mom or Dad. In the end, it didn't really matter as long as it wasn't both. Eventually, I decided to learn from my father. At least he'd remain calm.

My father drove us to a largely vacant strip-mall parking lot and cut the engine. "You ready?"

"Yes! Let's switch places!"

"No. Not yet."

I took a deep breath. The steering wheel and the pedals were singing out to me like Sirens. And like Sirens, they could lure me to crash on a rocky coast. But I didn't care. Luckily we were in the Valley. No coast here. Only strip-mall parking lots peppered with speed bumps and disaffected youths.

He pointed to the armrest. "This is the armrest."

"Right."

"This is steering wheel."

"Yup."

"This is side-view mirror. There one over there too, on other side. It show you side."

"Uh, I know."

"This is rearview mirror. It show you rear."

"Yes, I know."

"This is for window." He cranked the window down. "Window go down." He cranked the window up. "Window go up."

"Dad, I *know*. I've been in this car before, you know?"

"This how you lock door from inside. This how you unlock. Lock. Unlock. Lock. Unlock. Yes?"

"Yes."

"This is dashboard."

"DAD! I took driver's ed at school, you don't have to—"

"I review for you, Annie. No yelling."

"But I know all of this. There's no need to teach me. I passed the written test!"

"This show you speed. Mile per hour. But it also show kilometer per hour. You know kilometer? It metric. One mile about one and a half kilometer."

"DAD!"

"No yelling. This show you gas tank. Right now about one-fourth full. That mean three-fourth empty. You know what kind of gas to use?"

"It takes unleaded."

"Very good. Don't put diesel in it."

"Why would I put diesel in it?"

"Don't put diesel, Annie."

"I'm not going to put diesel in this car."

"Very bad, very bad."

"I know, Dad. *No diesel.*"

"This for engine heat. This tell you how far you go."

"The odometer. Yes. I. Know."

"It tell you in mile or in kilometer."

"Dad."

"This is gearshift. *P* mean 'park,' *R* mean 'reverse.' That mean to go backward."

I groaned. "Dad, seriously?"

"*N* is 'neutral.' If car break down, you put in neutral to push car, you know?"

"Yes. But I can't push a Volvo. It's two tons. *Metric* tons."

"*D* is for 'drive.'"

"Yes, drive, which is what I'm *not* doing right now."

"Then this first gear and second gear. We do that later."

"I know what they do. What does this do?" I pointed to a little slot next to the gearshift.

"I don't know. Look at manual."

"We can do that later."

"No, do now."

"Why do we need to do it now? It's not important. You don't even know what it is." I'd never felt so much regret in my entire life.

"Look in glove box. That is glove box over there."

"I know where the glove box is. We'll look it up later."

"Anne . . ."

"*Fine.*" I wrenched open the glove compartment and rifled through papers and melted pens to find the manual. It took a few minutes to thumb through it. "It's to lock the gearshift."

"Why we need to lock?"

"No idea. Maybe it's a German thing."

"Volvo is Sweden."

"Maybe it's a Swedish thing. You obviously don't use it."

"Still, good to know. This radio. You turn on and off like this."

"I know how radios work."

"This volume. You can go volume up or volume down."

"Dad. You're killing me, you murderer."

"This tape player. You can move ahead, called 'fast-forward,' and you can move back, called 'unwind.'"

"Actually . . . uh, never mind."

An hour later, he finally finished identifying the features in the inside of the car, including the vanity mirrors. He cautioned me never, ever to "check vanity" while I was driving. Then we got out of the car to review every part from the gas cap to the hubcaps.

"Okay, *now* do I get to drive?"

"No. You watch me drive first."

"I've been watching you drive my whole life, Dad. I have to try it."

"No. You watch and listen."

He drove us home. He narrated every single thing he was doing.

"Now I press on gas pedal. Not too hard because speed limit is thirty-five mile per hour. I go change lane now, so I turn on signal. I look at mirror, look over shoulder, look at mirror. I change lane now. See? I change lane. Smooth, one motion. Now speed limit is forty, so I push gas a little harder. You understand how to do it?"

"Not really. Dad, if I'm going to learn how to drive, I have to actually drive the car. You, like, get that, right?"

"So there red light ahead. I slow down. I release gas pedal slowly, slowly, I press on brake. We slow, slow, slow, slow . . . slow . . . . . . slow. Now we stop. You know light? Red mean stop, green mean go, yellow mean—"

"DAD!"

"No yelling. Yellow mean slow down. Some people speed through yellow, but that dangerous."

"You speed through yellow."

"Never."

"You speed through yellows all the time. Are you kidding me? *Everyone* speeds through yellows."

"Don't speed through yellow."

"Yes, yes, I know, I'm just saying you speed through yellows often. Don't lie."

We pass a gas station. "Remember, no diesel in car."

"Oh my God, are you joking?"

"Not a joke! No diesel, Annie!"

"I know!"

He pulls into our driveway and parks the car.

"Now do I get to drive?"

"No. Tomorrow, I give new lesson. You think about what you learn today."

"I didn't learn anything today."

"What? You learn about gearshift, remember? You find out Volvo from Sweden. You learn a lot, Annie. You just not know it. We drive tomorrow." He gets out of the car and closes the door. "You lock the door. You remember how to lock?"

The next day I found my dad reading at the kitchen table. I jiggled the keys to the car. "Let's go!"

He held up the car manual. "You read this?"

"Why should I read that?"

"To learn."

"I know everything there is to know. You taught me everything yesterday."

"Really? How much gas mileage does Volvo have?"

I was silent.

"Well? You know everything, so you tell me."

"Gas . . . mileage? Like . . . how many miles per gallon? Uh . . ."

He nodded. "Yes."

"Like, fifty?" I saw the look on his face and corrected myself. "No, I mean, like, twelve."

"Not even close. About twenty. You have lot to learn." He held up a tire-pressure gauge. "What is this?"

That I knew, thanks to my driver's ed class. "It's to check how much air you have in your tires."

"Not how much air, how much air *pressure*."

"Same difference."

"Not same. How much air you have and how much air *pressure* you have very different, Annie. How come you not pay attention in science? You understand *pressure*?" My dad was a scientist. I was a teenager, ergo, not a scientist. "How many mile before you need oil change?"

"You should get one whenever the light comes on."

My dad shook his head in disappointment. "When you rotate tire?"

"When your dad tells you to."

"Annie."

He launched into Driving Lesson #2: Caring for Your Vehicle. He taught me how to check the oil, the air *pressure* of the tires, and even the windshield-wiper fluid. The lesson lasted a few hours, during which I never turned on the engine.

The following day it was Driving Lesson #3: Underneath the Hood. He reviewed the battery, spark plugs, radiator, carburetor, various filters, and other parts that I quickly forgot about. I still don't know what a carburetor does, and I'm not afraid to admit it. Driving Lesson #3 also did not include any driving.

Then it was Driving Lesson #4: Scenarios Involving Inconvenience and Possible Danger.

Q: Suppose the taillight is out. What should you do?
A: Go to Jiffy Lube.

Q: Suppose the engine light comes on, what should
   you do?
A: Go to Jiffy Lube.

Q: Suppose the engine starts smoking. What should
   you do?
A: Stop driving. Duh.

Q: Suppose the battery is dead. How do you jump it?
A: Call AAA's twenty-four-hour roadside assistance
   from a call box. I'm totally not flagging down some
   stranger on the freeway. I mean, *seriously*, Dad.

Most of my answers were, of course, incorrect or offered insufficient information. But, to be fair, a trained mechanic or even Mr. Bjørn Volvo himself (if there is such a man) couldn't have provided a good enough answer to please my father.

Eventually I had to wait for Driving Lesson #7 to actually drive the goddamn car. But before that there was Driving Lesson #5: Safety and You, and Driving Lesson #6: Distractions That Put Others at Risk of Dismemberment and/or Death. The latter included a treatise against driving and eating Taco Bell. Both eating and driving require two hands, he explained, so you can't do both at the same time "unless you octopus," and if that were the case, you wouldn't be driving or eating tacos in the first place.

For the actual driving lesson, he drove us to an empty parking lot. This parking lot happened to belong to my high school. I was horrified. Sure, it was Sunday and it was highly unlikely that

I'd be seen, but there was still a small chance for big, big embarrassment.

"Why can't we go to the Vons parking lot? There's more space there."

"Too many people go to supermarket. We need empty space."

"Dad, that parking lot is huge, we can drive around behind the store."

"Annie, you want drive here or not drive at all?"

I had to think about it. I imagined the cheerleaders, the jocks, and the entire student-body government gathered around the parking lot and, like, totally ragging on my junior-varsity skills. They'd hear my dad drone on about the difference between the "seek" and "scan" buttons on the radio. *Oh my God,* they'd think, *Annie is such a loser, she doesn't even know how to use a radio.* Soon the rumors would spread through school and, of course, through the entire school district, and I'd become an outcast at lunch, relegated to eating with the dweebs not even cool enough for the band nerds (which was the group of friends I normally belonged to).

"Annie?"

But what if I didn't learn to drive? I'd be that dork who begs for rides to band practice in my senior year of high school. Mom would have to drive me to the prom. No, wait, I wouldn't even be asked to the prom. To get to school, I'd have to take the bus, with all the freshmen—those *children*—and even they'd have no respect for me. I'd probably sit in the front of the bus, the area reserved for the biggest social rejects, including the one who couldn't quite shake that one time in fourth grade when he sat in dog crap and everyone thought he'd shit his pants and he was forever labeled as a pants-shitter. I'd be sitting in the front row, right next to the withered, old bus driver. She and I would be besties and she'd go on and on about needlepoint, water retention, and her hammertoes.

"Annie."

"Yes. I'll drive, I'll drive here."

We swapped places and I strapped myself into the driver's seat. I took a deep breath and looked around the parking lot. Empty. I was safe, for now. I turned on the engine. I could feel the vibrations under my feet. The pedals felt surprisingly soft and squishy. It was magnificent. I felt free. I felt like an adult. "This is *sooo* RAD!" I let out a squeal.

"Good driver stay calm."

"Right, right." I took a deep breath. "I'm, like, so calm." I could feel my heart exploding through my eyeballs.

"Take foot off the brake and press gas. Be gentle."

The car lurched forward at what felt like a hundred miles per hour. "Oh *shit*!" I slammed on the brakes and the car screeched to a halt.

My dad shifted in his seat and shook his head calmly. "Gentle, Annie. Be careful."

"Sorry, I wasn't expecting that."

"Press on gas very soft . . . like Mommy teacup."

"Okay, got it." My mother has a collection of china that's so precious she doesn't even use it for guests. We've never actually used them. I pressed the gas lightly and the car moved forward very, very slowly. The odometer barely registered.

"Okay, now push harder. Just little."

The car sped up. "This is so sweet!" I squealed again. I pressed harder and the car zoomed forward. "Look! I'm driving!" I beamed. "Can I honk the horn?"

"No. Horn is not toy. Watch the road, Annie."

"I'm watching! I'm watching! Oh my God, I'm driving! Oh-my-God-oh-my-God-oh-my-God!" I squealed again. My dad winced in pain. Nothing cuts like a teenage girl's scream in an enclosed vehicle.

"Calm, calm. Good driver stay calm, remember?"

We practiced driving around the parking lot. Going down the lanes, using the signals, turning left and right, and going in reverse. Occasionally, my father reached over to adjust the wheel and we steered together. I averaged about ten miles per hour, which was appropriate since that was the speed limit of a parking lot. The second I inched over the limit, I was warned about following laws and being a good citizen who cared about the safety of everyone on the road, including pedestrians and cyclists. It's not about your speeding, he reminded me, it's about people dying.

An hour later I was practicing U-turns and three-point turns in the parking lot. Controlling the two-ton Beast quickly became natural. I had a successful career as a long-haul truck driver ahead of me.

"Now, park the car."

I put the car in park, right in the middle of the empty lot.

"No, Annie, park car *in the space.*"

"Oh. Right." I didn't remember my father explaining the finer points of parking. I'm sure he did, but I was thinking about far more important things, like what outfit would best match my car, or how, when the light was just right, Jason Priestley's eyes were the exact same shade of blue as the Volvo. *My* Volvo. I looked around and surveyed the lot. I was surrounded by empty space. Parking should be easy, right?

"Pick a spot."

I pointed to an empty spot to my right. "There." I turned on my signal and turned. Done. Easy.

"Look at the line, Annie."

I cracked open my door to look at the lines on the ground. I was directly on top of one. "Boo."

"If there car here, you be on top of it. Try again."

I pulled out of the space. Backing up required intense focus—

turning the wheel in the correct direction required trial and error. Mostly error. I kept braking and adjusting the wheel. Then I pulled up to another spot, this time to my left. I started turning.

"Stop. Signal!"

"Oh, right. Sorry." I clicked it on.

"Always remember signal."

"I remembered last time."

"Last time was last time. This time is this time."

I turned into the space. "Okay, I think I got it this time."

He shook his head. "No. You on top of line."

"Really?" I opened the door again for a closer look. Sure enough, I was in the middle of two spaces. "Shit!" I slammed the door.

"Don't slam."

"Sorry."

"You have to turn into one space." He held up one finger. "*One.*"

"I know, I know."

"Do again."

I tried again. And failed again. The car was parked at an awkward angle. "I messed up."

"Try harder. It very easy."

"I am trying harder! Maybe I can't see the lines well enough." I sat taller in my seat. The Beast was not a big car, but I was a small person—just under five feet. I scooted the seat a little closer to the pedals. I took a deep breath. "All right. I'll get it this time."

I tried yet again. And failed yet again.

"Annie, you have to learn to park before you can drive."

"You think I don't know that?" I started biting my nails.

"Both hands on wheel!"

"Sorry! Sorry!"

My hands gripped the steering wheel at nine and three o'clock.
I took a deep breath and gnashed my teeth. "Let's go again."

I clicked on my signal and checked my mirrors. I started to
turn into the space but then kept on turning until I had made a
U-turn into the spot. Into several spots, really. "SHIT! I hate this!"

"We go home. We can park another day."

"I really want to get this."

"Enough lesson. You need break."

I shook my head. "I know it's not hard. Everyone can do it."

"You have your whole life to drive. You can't do all one day."

"Yes, I can."

"No, you can't."

"If I don't learn to park, then I can't drive. And if I can't drive,
then my life will be totally ruined, all because I can't park this
stupid car." I stopped myself. "No, it's not a stupid car. I'm stupid.
I hate this!" I stopped myself again. "No, I don't hate this."

"You have to be patient. It take time." My father sighed and
pointed to the street. "Let's go to Vons. You drive."

"Really?" I wasn't expecting to actually drive somewhere on
my first day. "Seriously? Oh my God!" I squawked.

"Good driver not scream, Annie."

I slowly drove out of the parking lot and pulled out onto the
street. My heart was racing though the car was not. I was actually
driving, like a grown-up! Me behind the wheel! Taming a moving machine of metal, grease, and gears! Transporting humans
quickly and safely over long distances! Well, it wasn't that far. The
grocery store was just a mile or two away, but hey, I was still getting there faster than by foot. It was exhilarating. The wind was
blowing through my hair. Kind of. The speed limit was twenty-
five miles per hour. No one else was actually driving that. Cars
were passing me, so I sped up ever so slightly.

"Twenty-five, Annie. Twenty-five."

"Okay, okay. Sorry. I was trying to go with the flow of traffic."

"You flow at twenty-five mile per hour. What that in kilometer?"

"I don't know. I can't figure it out because I'm driving."

"Good answer, Annie."

I turned on my signal and began turning into the parking lot. But I overturned and headed toward the curb.

"Straighten! Straighten wheel!"

"I'm trying! I'm trying!"

With a heavy thump and a violent jerk, the front wheels rolled over onto the curb. Concrete scraped against the bottom of the car.

"SHIT! SHIT!"

I imagined the transmission falling out and the gas tank cracking. There'd be a long trail of nondiesel gasoline behind us, which would catch on fire. Just as the flames reached the engine, we'd leap out of the Volvo, narrowly escaping a fatal explosion. Then my father would say, "Yippee ki-yay, motherfucker."

"Sorry!"

With another thump and a jerk, the back wheels rolled over the curb and we coasted into the parking lot. I checked the rearview mirror to make sure I hadn't left a muffler behind.

"Be careful. Don't hit anything." He pointed to the cars and people with grocery carts.

"I'm not going to hit anything, I swear. I'm okay. I'm okay, right?"

"Park there." He pointed to a spot between two cars.

"No, I don't know. Maybe I should park somewhere else." Like in the middle of a field. "Let's go behind the store. No one parks there."

"Annie, park there."

"Maybe I should do something easier?"

"Annie."

I took a deep breath and turned on the signal. I slowly turned into the space, concentrating on pressing the gas lightly. I imagined myself flooring it accidentally and plowing into a group of seniors who, for whatever reason, were playing gin in the supermarket parking lot. I stopped. "I have to back up, I'm too close."

"No, keep turning wheel. Turn, turn, turn." He reached over and turned the wheel with me. "Now go."

I inched into slowly into the space. "Oh my God, I think we're going to hit that car. It's a Mercedes."

"Stop. Calm down."

"It's a Mercedes! They're like a million dollars."

"Annie, keep turning, keep turning."

"I think this car is too big for the space."

"Volvo is compact car, Annie. You know what compact car is?"

"I should back up. I want to start over."

"No, you fine. Keep turning."

I finally squeezed the Beast into the space. "Oh my God! Did I do it? Did I do it? Shit! I did it! I did it!" I jumped up and down in my seat triumphantly—or at least tried to. My seat belt held me back. I wanted to drive a victory lap around the grocery store and have my pit crew—my father—pour Gatorade over me.

"No." My dad frowned and looked out his window. "No. Too close to this car. How can driver get into his car if you right next to him?"

"But I didn't hit him."

The next few weeks were about drills, drills, drills. My father had created an elaborate lesson plan for teaching me how to park. He explained every step in excruciating—really excruciating—detail. Then he had me watch (and take notes) as he parked the car. Then he instructed me to watch other people park their cars at the mall (and take notes; I felt like a stalker). He even demonstrated the finer points by maneuvering household objects around the kitchen table. It looked something like this:

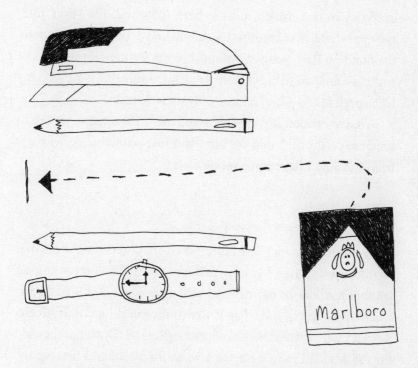

My father directed me to park to the left and then to the right of a single car, and then between two cars. He had me parking in spaces to my left and then to the right. We practiced parking in forty-five-degree-angle spots and ninety-degree spots. I parked next to oversized planters that invaded spaces, squeezed the Beast next to shopping-cart stalls, and maneuvered around columns.

I practiced parking in our garage and pulling out of our garage. Eventually I became comfortable. Parking became easy. In addition to long-haul trucking, I also had a successful career as a parking valet ahead of me. We eventually moved on to parallel parking with the same rigor.

The day after I turned sixteen, I took the road test and passed on the first try. I practically hugged every DMV employee who crossed my path and shared my thrilling, life-changing news with everyone in line, which must've been irritating. The DMV does not appreciate or encourage joy. In my first driver's license photo, the blinding flash washed out most of my features, so all you can really see are two wild eyes and a gigantic smile that is ripping my face apart. Like a Cheshire cat, only more Korean.

That afternoon my mother asked me if I wanted to go out to lunch to celebrate. I said yes but that I just wanted to go with my friends; could I have some money?

Some people say they left home when they went to college, but for me, it was when I got my driver's license. I could use the car without restrictions more or less, as long as I followed Rule #1: Say where you're going and when you're coming back, and Rule #2: Get A's in school. There was also, of course, Rule #3: Don't put diesel in the car. My dad passed me the keys to the Volvo and sent me off. In a way, my mother was also liberated. She was no longer chained to my schedule; her services as my personal driver were no longer needed. So she, too, left home. My father was never at home and always at the lab. My brother was already out of the house.

I shuttled myself to and from school, track practice, orchestra rehearsals, band competitions, and flute lessons. Turns out that without my mother, I was actually a punctual person. With a license I could take on babysitting jobs and tutoring jobs, volunteer at the hospital, and decorate Rose Parade floats. I took friends on vintage-shopping marathons, and I caravanned to the library, beach, bookstores, record stores, rock shows, and Disneyland. I served as the designated driver to house parties, and I pulled over whenever friends needed to hurl. I carpooled with friends to save money on gas and gave rides to stranded friends. I rarely ate with my parents, preferring instead to eat with friends at a twenty-four-hour café in Santa Monica where the sandwiches were named after news anchors. (My favorite was the Connie Chung.) I often came home late, pushing the boundaries of what was reasonable for a sixteen-year-old. My parents were not thrilled and most definitely worried, but I maintained a nearly perfect GPA, marred only by a B in AP chemistry, which my father balked at. I guess he thought chemistry was genetic. It's not, actually. My AP biology class taught me that.

The house was pretty much empty. My mother spent more time with friends and took on more responsibilities at her church. My father expanded his lab and sought out more work. We were ghosts, blurred images that darted across the house and into the garage. It was the days before we all had cell phones, so my mother and I began leaving notes for each other on the kitchen counter.

"Track meet 3–7, then going to Karen's for Spanish homework. Dinner with her. —Annie"

"Get milk, egg. —mommy"

"Band competition Saturday. Need money for gas. —A"

"We go church party. —mommy"

"I passed the AP Spanish test!"

"Grandma came today. You miss her. She miss you."

More often than not, I'd come home and there'd be plates of

lukewarm food wrapped in plastic and a place setting for me at the kitchen table. It was something my mother usually did for my dad whenever he came home late from his lab. Sometimes I'd come home and my dad would be sitting there eating dinner by himself. I'd sit down in my usual spot and we'd talk quietly so we wouldn't wake up my mother. Even if I had already eaten, I'd eat again. Other times, my mother would hear me come in and wake up. She'd shuffle into the kitchen in her nightgown and fix me something to eat, even though I insisted I could do it myself. As I ate, she'd peel an apple so it'd be ready for dessert by the time I finished.

My mother and I are heading to Koreatown for tofu hot pots. This time she is in the driver's seat. Despite my best efforts, she won. ("Sometime you lose, Anne. Grow up, baby!") We are cruising down the freeway, and traffic is moving freely, which does happen from time to time in Los Angeles. I'm not sure if she's aware of it, but my mother is veering inside her lane.

"Mom, watch the road."

"I watch it. Of course, I watch it." She looks at me incredulously, which means she is actually not watching the road. The car moves slowly to the left.

I point to a car passing to our left and pant helplessly. "Watch it, watch it, watch it."

"Watch what?"

I sit on my hands to prevent them from reaching over and taking control of the steering wheel. I can feel my fingers impulsively wriggle underneath my butt. Sometimes when my mother's behind the wheel, my feet actually mimic pushing on the pedals. I'm aware of it and I still can't stop myself.

Then, hundreds of feet in front of us, a car changes lanes. My mother steps on the brakes firmly. I lurch forward, the seat belt cutting into my collarbone. Then she guns the engine. I get thrown back. The seat belt pins my shoulders to the seat and locks in place as a safety measure. I yank at it futilely.

"MOM, DON'T BRAKE! Why are you braking?"

"Because someone change lane!"

"But there's plenty of space, you don't have to brake! Why would you brake?"

"You brake when someone change."

"Not if they're, like, a hundred miles in front of you."

"Not hundred mile, Anne."

"There was a ton of space. You were fine."

Soon we approach a busy interchange. I claw my armrests and brace myself for a collision that will no doubt end in an amputation of some kind. First, she speeds up going into the interchange. Then, as she merges with other cars traveling at top speed, she brakes.

"OH MY GOD!" I reach out to steel myself against the dashboard and hope we don't get hit, which would set off the airbag, which would break my wrists and all my fingers and obliterate my lifelong dream of becoming a timepiece spokesperson. ("Annie Choi. Writer. Role model. Timeless. Chooses Rolex." The ad would be black and white because that shit's classy.)

"HOLY FUCK, MOM, DON'T SLOW DOWN!"

"What?"

"DON'T BRAKE WHEN YOU'RE MERGING!"

"Why you yell?"

"OH GOD, WE'RE GOING TO DIE!"

Behind us people honk; some slam on their brakes too, and a few are able to swerve around us.

"Anne, we merge, so we slow down! Why you scream?"

"You're not supposed to slow down! Go at the speed of traffic, not slower. You're going to kill us!"

"Why I kill my only daughter?" She rolls her eyes. My mother is someone who rolls her eyes in the face of death, as opposed to normal people, who scream like banshees.

As people pass us, they give us the stink eye and mouth impolite remarks. I look extremely apologetic. My mother stares right back and throws up a hand, as if to say, *What? What did I do?* She shakes her head in disgust and outrage. I know what she's thinking: *No one can drive in this town.* This is, of course, what everyone in Los Angeles is saying at this very moment.

Now we are on another freeway. This one has traffic. However, the fast lane is moving. Naturally, my mother is not in that lane. She is in the lane farthest to the right, the slow lane. The slow lane gets its name because people use it to slow down and exit the freeway. We are not exiting. We are, however, slowing down.

"You should change lanes."

"No. We okay."

"But the fast lane's moving fast. Let's get in that lane. Then we'll get there faster because . . . it's faster. Do the math!"

She takes her hand off the steering wheel to brush me off, a dangerous move. "Go away."

"It's physics! Math! Time is equal to distance divided by rate. At this rate, it'll take hours to get there. Maybe even days."

"We get off at Normandie."

I glance at the freeway sign and sputter, "That's in eight miles!"

"It come very quick."

"But there's enough time to get into the fast lane and pass by all this bullshit!"

"Anne, you never get husband with you mouth."

"I bet any husband would drive in the fast lane."

"I bet you husband ride bus."

"Mom, it's the fast lane! Look at it! It's there just so we can use it. It wants us to use it. It's saying, 'Oh! Oh! Use me! I will set you free!'"

"Ayoo, Anne, *eep dah-doh."* This literally means "close your mouth." But what she really means to say is "shut the fuck up," except she doesn't curse, because she's a lady or whatever.

I am by no means a lead-foot. I've gotten tickets, yes, but I consider myself more of a "mover" than a speeder. To me, the whole idea behind driving is to move, and to continue to move until you arrive at your destination and you don't have to move anymore. My mother is not a mover. She is, in fact, the opposite. She's a braker. If she could, she'd go in reverse whenever anyone changed lanes. My mother fulfills several stereotypes of bad drivers: She's a woman, she's Asian, and she's older. She has three strikes against her. It occurs to me that when I drive, I fulfill most of the same stereotypes, but I brush that thought away. I'm not old, and I'm a good driver. No, really, I am.

We finally get to the off-ramp. We exit and now we are in street traffic. In Koreatown, the left-turn pockets at major intersections always get filled and cars spill out into the left lane, backing up traffic for blocks. Of course, we are in the left lane.

"Why don't you move into the right lane and go around this? Traffic is really bad."

"Because we turn left on Wilshire, so we stay on left side."

"But we don't have to turn for a few blocks."

"We turn soon."

"Mom, get in the other lane, and then drive a block or two past Wilshire to avoid all the turning traffic, and go down one of the smaller streets. Then drive around the block. It's a lot faster. That's what I do all the time."

"That take longer."

"No, it doesn't, I swear. I swear on my mother's grave."

"Anne, that how people get ticket."

"People don't get tickets for driving around the block. If anything they're *improving* traffic conditions. They should get awards."

"Like Oscar?"

"Yeah! Go around! Get the Oscar for Best Driver. You can be, like, the Meryl Streep of driving."

"What about Julie Robert?"

"Meryl Streep is better. Or how about Katharine Hepburn?"

"Oh, Mommy like her."

"Then drive like Katharine Hepburn!"

"She dead, Annie."

"Goddamn it, just drive past all this shit and go around the block!"

"You mouth!"

"I'll say worse things if you don't go around!"

Then our lane moves forward several cars.

"See? We move! Your way slower, Anne."

"That's because we've been arguing over actresses for an hour."

"Not hour. Five minute. And not argue. Discuss."

"I took creative license."

"Like driving license?" My mother laughs.

"Yeah, but you don't have to take a test to get it."

"Good, because maybe you fail!" She cackles and winks at me, which means, once again, her eyes are not on the road.

The light turns yellow and she guns the engine so she can pull into the intersection and make her left turn. But at the last minute, she decides, no, she won't make it, and slams on the brakes.

"Mom!"

"What?"

"If you're going to go for it, you have to go for it."

"No, too dangerous. Is that how you drive?"

"Yes."

"Who teach you to drive like that?"

"You know exactly who taught me. The question is, who taught *you* to drive like *this*?"

"You daddy."

It is one of those moments where something clicks and everything should make sense, but it doesn't. At all. It's as if a light has come on and instead of seeing things clearly, you see something totally bizarre and you say, "What the hell is *that*? Is that where that smell is coming from?" My mother and I both had the same teacher, and yet she is a bad driver. What does this mean? Maybe my mother is just a bad student? Then it occurs to me that my mother is a bad driver but thinks she's a good one. Does this mean I'm a bad driver but think I'm a good one? I begin to question myself. Am I a good student? Do I actually have nice hair? How's my breath? Then I stop. No, no, I'm a good driver.

Eventually, we make our left turn and pull into the restaurant parking lot. We made it alive, somehow.

"Your driving stresses me out."

"You drive make Mommy stress too."

"I'm glad we had this talk. Now let's get out of this stupid car, and I'll buy you lunch."

"No, you buy Mommy lunch."

"Woman, that's what I said!"

She slams the car door.

"Don't slam the door!"

Dear San Fernando Valley,

When people ask me where I'm from, I say I'm from Los Angeles. Then when they ask what part, I wince a little. I mutter "the Valley" and then I look apologetic, as if I've just delivered some disappointing news. It's the same look a waitress has when she tells you they're out of key lime pie. She's embarrassed. Helpless. A little sad, even. She can see the unsatisfied and unimpressed look on everyone's faces. The Valley, while still technically part of Los Angeles, is not the same. Beachy, wealthy Santa Monica or trendy, tattooed Silver Lake is not the same as Winnetka, a community in the 818 with several unlighted parks and a particularly understaffed and painful post office.

My dear Valley, I understand what you are and it's hard to feel proud. You are strip malls crammed with fast-food joints, discount shoe outlets, and a drive-through Starbucks. You are a giant, unshaded parking lot flanked by a T. J. Maxx, Best Buy, and a Bed Bath and Beyond. Practically every block has a check-cashing counter, the office of a personal-injury lawyer, and a guy spinning a sign to woo you into a cell phone store. He is very enthusiastic about rollover minutes. There are plenty of hair salons that promise "transformations," and they're down the street from salons that specialize in color correction. The Valley has too many tanning studios, which seem unnecessary in an area where UV is relentless and free. I know a place where you can get eyelash tints and extensions because your natural eyelashes are inadequate. I also know a place where you can get a Brazilian, a Thai massage, a lip piercing, and a colonic, though most likely from an unlicensed person. In the Valley, you can get hypnotized to stop smoking or lose weight or go to comedy traffic school. You can outfit your entire home from the 99¢ Only Store or buy gifts from a shop that sells books, swords, knives, and shoes (it says so right on the sign). There's a block in the deep V where you can rent a tuba, get "affordable and pain-free" dental care, and buy a fireplace. You can also play laser tag and get laser hair removal, though not at the same place. In *The Karate Kid,* Daniel-san and his mother move from Newark to Reseda. They basically didn't move, because the Valley is the New Jersey of Los Angeles.

For some reason, you love donuts and there are shops everywhere, all with unimaginative names: Donut Inn, Donut Stop, Donut Man, and the particularly vague Donuts & More. There are also Dad's Donuts, Mama's Donuts, and Uncle Joe's Donuts; it's a very wholesome family affair. There are hundreds of Chinese restaurants with "Empire" in their name and dozens of buffets that serve Mongolian beef, macaroni salad, and E. coli. The Valley is for half-priced sushi, Edible Arrangements, and convenience stores that are only convenient if you want to buy bottom-shelf vodka, chewing tobacco, and a single lime. It's for bars without windows, vacant retail spaces, and a strip club called the Candy Cat Too. Nobody knows where the original Candy Cat is.

You are the capital of adult entertainment and produce 90 percent of the world's porn. There's a bar where porn stars come and sing karaoke on Tuesday nights. Common people can sing too; my friend sang "Personal Jesus" and really killed it. When ever excessively busty ladies come into restaurants, people just shrug and eat their "oven-style" burritos in peace. It's just a part of life in the San Pornando Valley. The industry is seated in quiet, inconspicuous Chatsworth, which is actually where Gene Autry and Roy Rogers made their movies. It's also where Marilyn Monroe allegedly lounged by the pool with John F. Kennedy and where Joaquin Murrieta, the Mexican Robin Hood, hid in the 1850s after he fought and killed his wife's murderers.

Valley, you're easy to make fun of and hard to love. I have to remember that for every cash-for-gold "store" there's a Korean supermarket that gives candy to kids. I happen to adore candy. For every used-car lot with sagging balloon arches, there's a *carnicería* with racks of *obleas con cajeta,* which are wafers filled with caramel and cavities. There are Indian spice shops that sell frozen naan and Israeli grocers with impossibly creamy hummus. There are Thai markets where I learned what lemongrass looks like and Russian bakeries with bread the color of asphalt. You are a place where anyone and everyone can thrive. You are a synagogue next to a Chinese Christian church near a *botánica* that sells magical healing amulets—all behind a Guitar Center. You are where to go for the best vegan Vietnamese restaurant ever. It's unassuming and humble, which is how most things are in the Valley. Even when something's trashy, there's a modest air to it. Maybe it's the simplicity of a sign: CIGARETTES FOR LESS.

You, Valley, are for hardworking people who have nothing to prove, unlike Hollywood and its endless supply of tools. But you're also where celebrities grew up, live, or retire—Kevin Spacey, Joey from *Friends,* and Micky Dolenz of the Monkees, in that order. They all seem to shop at the Whole Foods at Riverside and Coldwater. I remember twice you tried to secede from Los Angeles County and become your own, more financially stable city. You would've become one of the largest cities in the United States. But the people voted it down. Everyone decided the Valley was fine just the way it is—a charmless, bland area of a flavorful city. There was no reason to change.

When I meet people from the Valley, there is a familiarity. We share the same affection and embarrassment, the way fans bond over a hopeless, losing team. We understand our roots; we share the same language. We grew up driving down Ventura or shopping in "Shoaks" (Sherman Oaks). My friend works in "Studes" (Studio City) and we go to the IKEA in "Burbs" (Burbank). NoHo is an area in Manhattan, but it's also one in the Valley: North Hollywood. There you can find a cemetery where Curly from *The Three Stooges* is buried. It's not too far from many Targets.

I want to say thank you, Valley. Thank you for providing my adolescence with your many malls and their bountiful food courts. Thank you for your lowered Hondas that speed past me on the 101, the 405, and the 134. Thank you for the relatively traffic-free 170, which is useless because it doesn't go where I want to go. I'm sorry you'll never be as quaint as Los Feliz or as sparkly as West Hollywood, and I'm sorry you'll always be ten degrees hotter than downtown. But I realize you couldn't care less. You are happy with what you are—you embrace your shady auto body shops just as much as your cardio-ballet studios. You don't aspire to be anything but yourself, even though you are the overly tanned butt of countless jokes. But in all this, you can always take comfort in one thing: At least you're not Orange County.

Your Valley Girl,
Annie

WHEN DISASTER STRIKES

I am heading southbound on the 101, going downtown. I am driving a rental car, a late-model Chevy the same color and size as a walnut. My car struggles to sustain sixty-five miles per hour, and other cars cruise past me. Amazingly, there is no traffic. I flip through the radio mindlessly. I settle on the oldies station, and it plays a steady stream of eighties hits, making me feel old. I am insulted; you cannot put Chubby Checker in the same category as Duran Duran. Coming around a gentle curve, the late-afternoon sunshine strikes the windshield, blinding me for a moment. When my eyes adjust, I see a field of red brake lights around the 405 interchange. I slam on the brakes and hear the sound of forks scraping across a chalkboard. I glance in my rearview mirror to see a black SUV speeding toward me, its windshield flooded with sunlight. The image in the mirror grows bigger and bigger at an alarming pace. I hear no screeching wheels. There is no sign that it's slowing down.

$$\bullet \bullet \bullet$$

I am on a bus zipping down a narrow, twisting road. It is raining. A yellow sign states the obvious: SLIPPERY WHEN WET. Another delivers a warning: WATCH FOR FALLING ROCKS. I frown. When rocks fall, there's not much you can do (other than watch them), so why bother calling attention to them in the first place? It is unnecessarily stressful. I am stressed. No one else seems to care. The bus is returning from a high school field trip. Josh and Jen are, like, totally making out in the back. Sam is air-drumming and arguing over who is better, Metallica or Led Zeppelin, and don't even talk to him about Phish, those dirty hippies. Nearly everyone is copying my Spanish homework. Señora García will be surprised to learn that her entire class wants to *"visitar Corea el próximo verano."* The air hangs heavy with hair spray and mint gum. Lightning fractures the sky and I start counting the seconds until I hear thunder. Suddenly, the bus hydroplanes. It swerves left, then right, then left again. The bus fishtails across the center divide and into oncoming traffic. It happens so quickly there is no time to scream.

I am on the A train heading uptown. I stifle a yawn and bemoan the asshole we call morning. The woman sitting to my left painstakingly applies mascara with a caterpillar on a stick. The man to my right rustles a copy of the *Times*. I'm sneaking glances over his shoulder to read the headlines when I catch his eye. He turns away from me and folds the paper into a small, tight rectangle. I look at my shoes instead and realize the laces are untied and dragging on the filthy subway-car floor. The train begins to speed up into a turn and the standing passengers lean and stagger to the right. A girl in nosebleed heels curses when she spills her venti coffee all over her sweater. The train speeds faster and faster, roaring louder and louder. Then the car lurches. There is a deafening screech of metal on metal. The car spasms and swings wildly, catapulting passengers down the aisle. People cry out, but they can't be heard over the screaming tracks. The lights flicker until they turn off and the floor roars below us. I begin floating out of my seat and my hands grasp at the air for something to hold.

None of these things have actually ever happened to me. I've never been in a car accident (when I was the driver). My buses always arrive safely, though perhaps not always on time. My subway rides are uneventful, save service cancellations, delays, and the occasional vagrant yelling racist slurs and demanding spare change. Takeoffs and landings have always been smooth, train rides have been unexceptional, and I've never been on a submarine. Boats always rock me to sleep, and I often wake up with my head pitched forward and drool pooling at the sides of my mouth. But, you know, in a sexy way. Nevertheless, I think about destruction and calamity whenever I'm driving, flying, or riding anything, be it a bike or a funicular. Actually, I think about catastrophes all the time. I think about fires in my apartment, cave-ins at my office, and tornados at the deli. I think about falling off cliffs, falling down manholes, and once I was in the middle of a gang shootout.

Once I survived a fire with third-degree burns covering 42 percent of my body.

Once I came down with Rocky Mountain spotted fever.

Once I got chased by bees and won.

Once I got chased by bees and lost.

I shot a bear.

My situations conclude in various ways, ending in a miracle or in death or something in between. Sometimes, I'm left paralyzed from the waist down, but I'm still alive and I get to drive one of those minivans with the gas and brake pedals on the steering wheel. Obviously, my minivan would be bright blue and green and it would say "Mystery Machine" on the side. In other cases, I am left in a mostly vegetative state and family members argue over whether or not they should pull the plug since I am occasionally responsive. Sometimes, I walk away from an extraordinary accident with nothing but an inch-long cut above my eyebrow, the kind George Clooney might get in an action movie. Nothing that scars a Hollywood face. I've lost fingers while making smoothies, fixing lawn mowers, and trapping caimans on the Amazon. I've lost toes by chopping wood and lifting a car off an ugly puppy. I've lost my eyesight, the ability to speak, and/or all of my teeth. My mother finally stops complaining that I never listen to her when I lose my hearing.

In the event of my death, all of my money would go to my family, and they would be confused. They'd think, *Surely there is another bank account with thousands of dollars; how could she have survived on $13.82?* Dealing with my "estate" wouldn't be too hard since I don't own much. My books would be donated to public libraries and my computer equipment given to an inner-city school, even though my brother would probably want it. My zombie and cannibal movies would go to Larry and Perri, who were the ones who got them for me in the first place. I'd leave Marc and Lizzie all the food left in my refrigerator because they'd cook something tasty with it, even though there'd just be ketchup and a bag of frozen edamame (which I use for sprains). Rosalyne would care for my stuffed animals. Eventually someone would uncover a stash of vintage New Kids on the Block Trapper Keeper folders that I bought in 2003. I bargained the store manager down to $4.75 from $20 for the entire case. Friends would remember my overdeveloped sense of irony and shed tears and then fight over the folders because they are awesome. Any journals or diaries found during the liquidation of my life would get buried with my body so that no one would ever read them.

A few years ago, the aerial tramway that runs between Manhattan and Roosevelt Island broke down. About seventy people were suspended in a metal shoebox high above the East River. Rescue workers managed to get the children and elderly off after a few hours. The rest had to wait for over ten hours; the last passengers weren't rescued until dawn. I remembered this incident while I was riding on the tramway, viewing the tops of Manhattan's skyscrapers at eye level. I wondered how I'd react if I were stuck there, the shoebox slowly swinging in the wind. The first thing that came to mind was where I'd go to the bathroom. I have a small bladder. I figured I'd pee in the corner, asking a fellow passenger to hold my coat around me to block my plumbing. Then I wondered if I'd survive the 250-foot drop and if the trolley would float in the East River, with its pollution and stench of dead fish. Ultimately, I decided it was possible to survive the drop, but the trolley wouldn't float. I imagined who'd be trapped in the car with me (a mother with a stroller, an investment banker, a Chinese food delivery guy, and a rabbi—typical New Yorkers). We wouldn't be able to wrench open the doors as the car sank into the river. We'd try kicking through the windows without success. Water would be leaking in from all sides, and it'd be full of mercury and raw sewage and hypodermic needles. The water would also be really cold because, of course, this would happen in the dead of winter. Passengers would be weeping good-byes into their cell phones, and at least one would be in a mindless panic and require a punch to the neck (the i-banker, probably). I'd call my family, but no one would pick up. So, I'd leave a message: *Hi, Mom, this is Annie, I'm sinking in the East River. I'm about to die. I just wanted to say I love you and sorry for breaking that sugar bowl, and once I lied about having cramps so I could take Grandma's Vicodin recreationally— okay, that was more than once, and—*

"We've now arrived at Roosevelt Island. Please watch your step while exiting. You can transfer here for the F line and the 101, 60, and 32 buses. Thank you for riding MTA New York City Transit."

Damn. A perfectly good disaster thwarted again.

I'm not sure exactly when I started daydreaming about catastrophes, but if I had to guess, I'd say shortly after the Northridge earthquake in 1994. I was in high school, and my brother was living at home while attending a junior college.

I woke up at dawn to our entire house shaking. At first it was just a rumble. I lay in bed with the comforter around my shoulders, my eyes wide and my body tense. I had been in earthquakes before, and they're usually over before you even realize what's happening. But I quickly saw that this one was different. The shaking was angrier, more aggressive. Some earthquakes feel as if the ground is rolling underneath you; others have more jerking and thrashing. This had both. I assessed my options. Should I dash across the room and take cover under my desk? Should I get in a doorway? Should I just lie there in bed helplessly and hope for the best? As the shaking got worse, it became obvious I was in a horrible spot. A tall wooden bookshelf trembled near my bed, teetering precariously and spewing its contents onto the floor.

I jumped out of bed and darted to the safety of the doorway. "*Mom, Dad! Mike!* We're having an earthquake!"

"No shit!"

"*Mike!* You okay?"

"I'm okay!"

"*Mom! Dad!* Are you okay?"

"We okay, Annie!"

"I'm okay! We're okay!"

My curios were flying off the shelves. Porcelain animals, rocks from Yellowstone National Park, and a cup of seashells came down in a crash. Then came the books: *Beowulf, The Adventures of Tom Sawyer,* various Dickenses and Brontës. Elsewhere in the house, I could hear vases and dishes shattering on the tile floor. My mother had a small cast-iron replica of a bell at Bulguksa, a Buddhist temple in Korea, and it was ringing furiously, telling us it was time to pray. The walls were rumbling deeply, angrily. Furniture was clattering. The roof was booming. The entire house was going into a seizure.

"It's not stopping!"

No one could hear me over the thundering wood and breaking glass. The shaking was getting worse. My jewelry box fell over, and for a split second it rained gold and rhinestones. My lamp took a nosedive to the floor, and my alarm clock slid behind the nightstand. My windows were rattling loudly and dresser drawers were shaking out. Boxes were falling from the shelf in my closet in a series of heavy thuds. The earth was trying to swallow us. This was it, I thought, this was the Big One, the one I had learned about in school. This was how I was going to die, how we were all going to die—me, my brother, my parents, and everyone in California. I braced myself in the doorway and squeezed my eyes shut.

And then, it stopped.

It was hard to tell at first. My knees were still shaking. My knuckles had turned white from holding on to the doorjamb with a death grip. It was over. We weren't dead. We had survived. My underpants were dry. The quake had lasted twenty seconds, though it felt like hours. Everything seemed still and quiet, save my mother's car. The alarm was going off furiously.

I reached for the light switch, but the power was out. Our neighborhood was on an anemic grid; we often had power outages in the summer when too many people were running their air conditioners. Of course we'd have no power after an earthquake. Still, in the early-morning light I could see the destruction of my bedroom.

"Is everyone okay? I'm okay! Mom? Dad? Mike?" I tried not to panic.

"We okay!" my parents called out. "Mike?"

"I'm okay. I'm still in bed."

"We in bed too. Anne, where you?"

"I'm in the doorway."

"You're in the doorway?" My brother was incredulous.

"Anne? You in doorway? Where you going?" My mother was confused.

"You're supposed to go to a doorway during an earthquake."

"Really? Who tell you that?" Now my dad was confused.

"I learned it in school. Where else?"

"They teach you that in school?"

"Yes, Dad."

"In science class?"

"I don't know, does it matter? We have drills every semester. Mike, why aren't you in the doorway?"

"Because I'm in bed."

"What if something falls on you?"

"Most accidents happen when you run around during an earthquake. You're supposed to stay put. Like, you know, in bed?" I could feel the authority and exasperation in his voice.

I felt a sharp jab in my foot and realized I was stepping on one of my mom's broken Catholic tchotchkes that had fallen off a shelf outside my bedroom. I examined the bottom of my foot—nothing too bad, just a small cut. In the dawn light I could see a little bloodstain on the off-white carpet. My mother was going to flip out.

"Wow. So much shaking! I bet it was an eight point oh," my dad said.

My brother scoffed. "That's impossible. If it were an eight, we'd be dead."

"Maybe seven point five?"

"Our house is still standing, right? Maybe a five."

"No, Mike, more than five."

"Why are we arguing over this?" I asked, agitated. Only in my family would we argue over an earthquake right after an earthquake, instead of hugging like normal families. No one had even bothered to get out of bed. Well, except for me.

My mother chimed in. "Mike, I think you right. Maybe six."

"No, Mike wrong. It close to eight. Believe me."

"Dad, when did you become an earthquake expert?"

My father believes he's an expert on all things science just because he's a scientist. But he's a chemist. He could tell you everything about hydroxides, but he can't tell you much about blind-thrust faults or the difference between an earthquake's magnitude and its ground acceleration. But he thinks he can, and that's what matters. My brother reads a lot but has a tendency to mishear

things or hold on to "facts" that have changed or proven different more recently. So, my brother always thinks that my dad is
wrong, and my dad always thinks my brother is wrong. I happen to think both my dad and my brother are always wrong. My
mother chooses sides depending on whom she wants to annoy
that particular minute.

Then the earth rumbled again. The aftershock sent more items
cascading off the shelves.

"Holy crap!"

"Anne, are you okay?"

"I'm okay! Are you guys okay?"

"We okay! Mike, you okay?"

"It's just an aftershock. Everyone, just calm down. We're all
okay. We're not gonna die!"

"How do you know?" I whimpered loudly.

"Annie, it's an earthquake. There's nothing you can do about
it! It's not even a big one. Just chill out!"

The shaking stopped. But my entire body was still trembling.

"Dude, we need to turn off the car alarm, it's going to go on
and on."

"The keys are in the kitchen," I croaked. I could picture the
car keys on the kitchen counter, under a pile of pots, dishes, and
knives.

"I think that was five point oh," my father said, marveling.

"No, it wasn't, Dad."

I could feel my brother roll his eyes in the dark. In the movies, everyone escapes into the basement during a twister and they
huddle around a radio together. Not us. In a movie about our
family, we'd be arguing over which station to listen to and why
the reception was so lousy, and did someone forget to replace the
batteries, and stop hogging the blanket, Annie.

Aftershocks continued throughout the morning. Some were strong jolts and only lasted a second or two. Others were more drawn out but mild-mannered. A few felt just as severe as the first quake. After particularly bad ones, we'd check in to see if we were all okay. At one point I cautiously retrieved a pillow and a blanket from my bed and set up camp in my doorway. I was four years old again, scared of the dark, too proud to admit fear. I managed to find my backpack and grab my Walkman to listen to the radio. The only thing that came on was the prerecorded classical station, which was broadcasting from another city. I stayed awake the entire morning, trying to stay calm. I wondered about my friends and my relatives. I wondered about my grandma, though she lived pretty far away. I wondered if my high school had been destroyed, though I figured probably not with my luck. I wondered if my teachers were okay and whether classes would be canceled. I wondered about my Korean school, even though I had stopped going three years ago. An eccentric family up the street had peacocks, and I wondered about them. What about the Crockers and the Bowers? What if we were the only surviving family in the neighborhood?

I could hear my brother snore, which gave me some comfort. He was obviously not worried, so why should I be? But I was. I started creating situations. What if the roof caved in? How long could I live while I waited for people to dig me out? How much air would I have? How would I get water? What if my parents got buried; how would Mike and I get them out? What if they were all buried except for me? Through the early hours of sunlight, I tracked escape paths to my windows and to my brother's and parents' bedrooms. I kept a mental note of major obstacles that might be in my way. I tried to remember where the closest pairs of shoes were. We didn't wear shoes in the house, so it was more complicated than I thought. I had a pair of patent-leather vintage heels in my closet somewhere. They were painful but better than walking on Jesus tchotchkes. I imagined myself traversing the destruction of the neighborhood. What would I eat if I got hungry? Would I resort to cannibalism? After some thinking, I decided, yes, I would, and I'd eat the thigh first. Or maybe the arm. But definitely not the fingers. Not exactly filling.

After fiddling with my Walkman, I managed to find a working AM station. But I was quickly disappointed. No one had any information. No official reports had been released, so the DJ was just hazarding guesses, like my brother and my father. No one could call in because most of the phone lines were down, and the DJ recommended that people with service avoid using their phones to keep the lines free for emergencies only. So he just kept yammering without any real information, filling up airspace, and I ended up pressing play on the cassette, which I immediately shut off. It was Nine Inch Nails, which is the music that plays when someone with a knife is chasing you.

Later that morning, we assessed the situation. Our house was fine. There was a network of cracks in the floors and plastered walls, but not in the foundation, at least according to my father, who, in addition to being a chemist and a seismologist, is also an architect and structural engineer. Ceramic tiles in our hallway floor were loose and looked like a Scrabble board that had been jostled. We lost a lot of dishes, which my mother didn't like anyway, and a lot of tchotchkes, which I didn't like anyway. For the first time ever, we were allowed to wear shoes in the house, though my mother cringed whenever she saw our sneakered feet walking on the carpet. While we cleaned up, we commented on all the stupid crap we had, occasionally feeling remorse for the smashed trophy won in kindergarten or the shattered crystal fruit bowl. In the rubble of my bedroom, I found things that I had lost—a folder of letters from pen pals, a pin from my grandmother, a small finger puppet of a mouse that looked so real it freaked out my mother. I found old photos of my elementary school buddies and me. It was kind of fun to find long-lost friends and then put them back on the shelves, knowing that I'd lose them again. Maybe I'd find them during the next earthquake. Occasionally an aftershock jiggled items off the shelves again, and I waited for my guts to settle down before putting them back.

The garage was more or less the same—in disarray. Somehow the wonky metal shelves full of tools and drills hadn't tipped over onto our car. My father was relieved ("It like miracle!"). He'd imagined the chain saw crashing through the windshield. My brother carried the car keys on his belt loop and whenever a tremor set off the alarm, he dutifully turned it off.

My father was worried about his lab. He had a lot of chemicals there. The kind that eat through metal and melt people. Though his office was over twenty miles away in Burbank, the quake might have affected his work. Maybe the building had collapsed. Maybe power outages had caused safety measures to malfunction. Maybe the whole thing was on fire. Maybe there were chemicals combining into a toxic soup, leaching into the ground, affecting the locals and turning them into mutant superorganisms with an appetite for human flesh, which apparently I also have a taste for.

"Give me car key, Mike."

"Where are you going?"

"To lab."

"Dad!" I looked up from my broom and dustpan. "You can't do that."

"I have to check damage, Annie."

"But what if there's a big earthquake on the way there? We have to stick together."

"Worst over, Annie."

"How do you know?" I shook my head. "You don't know."

"I have to see lab. What if acid get everywhere?"

"So you're going to go into a room full of acid?"

"Annie."

"Dad. What if the roads are out?"

"Then I come back."

"But you don't know which roads are out, so what if you drive into a big hole?"

"I drive slowly."

"Mom . . ."

She frowned. "Maybe you should stay here with us." They talked in Korean, and I interrupted where I could.

"Annie, it fine. I go right there and come back. I just check and make sure everything safe there."

"What if we get separated? That'd be horrible. You can't call us. No phone."

"I said, don't worry. Maybe Burbank have no damage."

"Maybe it has a lot of damage."

"Annie. Enough. It take one hour. I come right back. Promise."

"You can't promise that. This is irresponsible!"

He walked out of the house and my heart seized. Both my father and I imagined a worst-case scenario, one filled with molten sludge. But while I preferred to avoid it (and instead just think about it and agonize), my father was driving toward it to experience the toxic apocalypse firsthand. If he even came back, he certainly wouldn't be the same. Maybe he'd be missing a foot. Or, conversely, I could see him with something extra, like a tail.

"It'll be fine, dude. Freeways were built to withstand all this shit." My brother shrugged. "Look, if it sucks out there, he'll come right back."

We continued to clean the rest of the afternoon. Though we didn't have power, our gas and water were somehow unaffected. My mother wanted to put together a few meals before all the food in our refrigerator rotted. She hated when food went to waste.

"OH MY GOD! OH NO!"

I heard her cries while I was cleaning up the living room. I bolted to the kitchen, stumbling over broken tiles. "What! Are you okay? What happened?"

She was doubled over the counter. She looked pained, as if someone had roundhouse-kicked her in the stomach.

"What is it?"

She silently opened the door to the pantry.

A Costco-sized jar of spaghetti sauce had fallen off a shelf. Red was dripping and oozing everywhere. Bits of onion and mushroom and bell pepper were sliding down the walls and collecting into chunky, thick pools. On the floor, sauce had seeped into every crevice in the cracked tile. It was a volcanic eruption of Mount Ragù, Old World Style. A sickening sweet and acidic stench grabbed my nose. "Oh God. That *is* bad."

"It go . . . everywhere. I thought maybe something die in there."

I laughed. "What would die in there? It'd have to be big to make a mess like that."

"Maybe whale?"

"Why would a whale be in our pantry?"

"Because he hungry."

"Oh crap, it got into the rice."

My mother groaned. "Oh no, no, no, no!"

Rice. The staple. During the apocalypse, rice would get us through. Not now. My mother rarely closed the large rice container tightly because she used it so much. Now the lid had flown off and shards of glass were nestled in the rice, covered with tomato sauce.

"Waste. Such waste." She handed me a sponge and a roll of paper towels.

We cleaned in silence. My mother is a big fan of buying in bulk. Oversized jarred and canned goods lined the shelves. I worried that they'd fall on us during a severe aftershock.

"Let's put the big stuff on the floor."

"Big stuff go on number four shelf." My mother shook her head. Things had a place.

"Well, now it can go on number zero shelf—the floor."

"No."

"What about the soy sauce?" It came in a large metal can, kind of like a gasoline container. "If that fell on your head, you'd be out cold."

"Why I be cold?"

"No, I mean you'd be in a coma."

"You silly. Number four shelf." She pointed up.

There was a gentle rumble under us and I froze. I immediately thought of my father. What if the road gave out underneath him? I shook off the thought. He probably hadn't even felt that one in the car.

"*Ayoo.*" My mother found a large mound of sauce in the mixer.

As we cleaned up the last of the mess, I heard the door open. My father had come home. I was relieved. He was alive, with both feet intact and no tail, not one that I could see anyway.

"Everything okay?" My mother sighed in relief.

"Everything fine. Broken glass, but all chemical good. I move everything I can under the table."

"That was smart." I nodded in approval. "See, Mom? He put the heavy stuff on the floor."

She ignored me.

"I think Burbank not too bad. Phone work a little." My father rattled off the list of people he had contacted successfully, including my grandmother and aunt, who lived downtown, over thirty miles away from us. My mother felt better. She cleared off a chair and sat down, exhausted.

"What about the roads?" I asked. "What about the neighborhood?"

My dad's eyes darkened. "Not too good. A lot of damage."

We all fell silent.

"I'm sure everyone's fine. If we made it, I'm sure everyone else made it, right? It wasn't that bad." I tried to convince myself.

"So many trees and lights fell down, but I think houses okay. I don't know where center was. It could be far away. Maybe Sylmar."

The Sylmar earthquake had happened before I was born, but we had learned about it in high school.

He paused and sniffed the air. "You make spaghetti?"

The U.S. Geological Survey reported that the epicenter was in Reseda, about eight miles away from our community. The main quake registered 6.7 on the Richter scale, so both my father's and brother's predictions were off. The ground acceleration was among the highest ever recorded in North America. The aftershocks were hardly mild. Some registered over 6.0 and a few of them occurred hours later, after most people thought the worst was over. Some reports showed over a thousand aftershocks in the area, though many were small and more or less imperceptible. But the aftershocks, I learned later, were deadly. The main quake weakened a lot of buildings and roads, and the aftershocks finished them off. When we got power two days later, we saw the buckled freeway interchanges and the sandwiched buildings on TV. Since Northridge suffered extensive damage, the earthquake was more or less named after the city. I watched the news in horror. Northridge was where we went to the mall, went shopping for Korean groceries, got haircuts, and bought chewy rice cakes filled with chestnut paste. I recognized crumbled streets and demolished buildings on the news. They were places I drove by practically every day or joints where I got frozen yogurt or used records. The Korean bakery that made fried buns stuffed with potato and carrots was no more. My heart sank. I couldn't watch and I couldn't stop watching.

Soon, the stories started coming in. Friends had lost their cars to fallen trees and telephone poles. Friends of friends had lost their family businesses or their homes. Many had lost their dogs and cats, though a few did return on their own days later. I found out that my flute teacher's apartment had extensive damage and had been condemned. Her building was on the front page of the paper. She decided to move to Ventura County and I stopped taking lessons altogether. My mother learned one of her fellow church members had died in an apartment building collapse. Her body was found in the closet.

"We very lucky, Anne." My mom nodded sadly.

Weeks after the earthquake, I stirred at every tremble in the house. If a truck rumbled past, I woke up. If wind rattled the windows, I woke up. If my brother snored extra loudly, I woke up. I kept a flashlight and a bottle of water on my nightstand and a pair of socks and shoes nearby. Sometimes I lay awake for hours, listening for the deep grumble of an earthquake, gripped in the unknown. After the earthquake, a few buildings had caught on fire, and I imagined our house engulfed in flames, embers of our bodies floating away like dandelion seeds. Then I thought of other disasters—landslides, floods, and avalanches. Then came tsunamis, hurricanes, limnic eruptions, and the occasional solar flare. Sinkholes gobbled our house and quicksand slurped up the entire street. Each night, I worked my imagination up until I was the only person left on the planet, or at least in the Valley. I roamed through Van Nuys, avoiding packs of wild dogs and scavenging food from AM/PM mini-marts while I journeyed to Santa Monica. Rumor had it that Santa Monica had shelter for Valley refugees.

While meditating on disasters, I've come up with a lot of tough questions. Could I start a campfire without matches if I were lost in the forest? Could I build a shelter in an ice storm? Could I cut off my own foot if it got caught under something? The answer to those questions is no. I'm not very handy. I don't have a good grip on physics and I tend to avoid sharp objects. It would take me five minutes to perish if I were stranded in the Australian outback. I can't even last five minutes at Outback Steakhouse. Look at me, I sit all day. In fact, I'm sitting right now. I'm ill-prepared to help during a true emergency. I don't know CPR, I'm too squeamish to put a dislocated shoulder back into its socket, I don't know how to leap out of a moving vehicle, and I can't lift anything heavier than a gallon of milk. I'm bad with a hammer, so you shouldn't hand me the jaws of life and say, "Help that baby out of the car wreck." It's not going to happen, my friend. My left knee clicks when I walk, and I have a horrible sense of direction. I'd get lost looking for help. I suppose I could yell for help. I'm good at yelling. I'm just not the kind of person who'd survive a catastrophe.

In the movie version of my life, I'd be the person who dies in the first few scenes.

I think this is why I enjoy thinking about disasters. I live a very low-adrenaline and low-carb lifestyle. I vacuum regularly. I like salad. My life is pretty mundane. Of course, I am grateful that my life is blissfully uneventful and stable. I have food and clean water and access to health care, and there are no land mines on Spring Street. I've got all my limbs and I can touch my toes, of which I have ten. But these daydreams help me realize how little control I have over life. I can get up in the morning, make my coffee exactly how I like it, and plan exactly where I'll go for dinner. I know what book I want and all the spots where I can buy it. I know where to get the best spanakopita in the city. But all that can change with a shift of the tectonic plates or a cyclone or a pandemic. After all, shit happens. I think Aristotle said that. Five-alarm fires, free-falling elevators, and electric eels help me put everything into perspective, which means realizing that I am helpless and it is an absolute miracle that I am alive and there is no good reason why I should continue being alive, and perhaps tomorrow I'll die and I don't have control over that, so really, why don't I just relax and maybe I'll bake a pie and hope my oven doesn't poison me with carbon monoxide.

Dear "A Guy,"

It seems like everyone knows you. But I guess this is no surprise. You're a genuinely likable person who's eager to help. You have at your disposal a variety of skills that the rest of us don't have the time or will to learn. You are a guy who can retile the bathroom, install shelves in a closet, or build a bookcase for an odd spot in the living room. You are a guy who can rewire that broken outlet so now we can finally blow-dry our hair in the bathroom. You are a guy who can fix the garbage disposal and discover there's a tea bag tangled around the blades. You once trapped a possum that came in through the doggie door and "dealt with it." You are a guy who has a drill. Also a sander, an angle grinder, and a sump pump. You have a jigsaw too, but I don't really know what that is. You are a guy with a truck who can take me to IKEA to buy a couch—speaking of which, are you available next Sunday afternoon?

You are a guy who can build a website or design business cards. You are a lawyer who can write a nasty letter to a landlord. You are a doctor who can write a prescription when I'm sick and have no health insurance. You know someone who might have freelance work for me. You can fix my computer and yell at me about backing up. You are good with cars. You are a bartender who'll hook my friend and me up with drinks. You are a great chef—you even roast your own coffee! You're also an Eagle Scout. You play drums. You were in a dog food commercial. You can get people a good deal on a flat-screen TV, a new laptop, a used car. You can get us into a time-share in Cancún, a house on Fire Island, a cabin in Tahoe. You have recommendations for London, Hong Kong, Chicago, or Berlin because you used to live there. You have a car in New York City, which means you have an impressive collection of parking tickets underneath the passenger seat.

I heard you got hit by a car while you were riding your bike, but you're okay. I heard you were in a car accident and flew through the windshield. It happened a long time ago, but you still have scars. I heard you had Hodgkin's but you're fine now, after the chemo. Someone told me you fell on a table saw and had your fourth finger attached to where your index finger used to be. Another friend told me you went rock climbing and fell off a mountain. You had to get helicoptered out. Someone told me you spent time in jail for drugs, or maybe it was embezzlement. Either way, I heard you're a guy who can get weed. I heard you drank so much you were rushed to the hospital and medics had to restart your heart. Then you went to AA and then later went to AA again. I also heard that you were never quite the same after you took acid in college.

You are a guy with parakeets named after talk-show hosts (Oprah, Oz, Dr. Phil). You have a dog that will bow if you say, "Hail, Satan!" You have a three-foot-long monitor lizard named Lucy that bit you on the cheek when you tried to give it a kiss. I'd like to remind you that reptiles are not capable of love. They leave their eggs behind because they have better things to do than rear their children. You told me that an octopus the size of a large pizza could squeeze into a crack that's the size of a dime.

Anyway, my friends said that you could help me out. I need a guy who can build a table. Is this something you can do? Doesn't need to be fancy, though it does need at least three legs. I've discovered that tables with two legs don't work very well. Also, I would like the top to be flat, preferably a rectangle or circle. Square is good too, but any geometry teacher will tell you that a square is just a type of rectangle. Wood is fine, but no wicker, please. Wicker is for people who enjoy humiliating trees. Of course, I'm more than happy to pay for materials and your time. My friends said your rates were reasonable and you were honest and skilled. They also said something about the time you walked from New York City to Baltimore—or maybe it was that you taught kite-surfing in Thailand. They could've gotten you confused with another guy.

Talk to you soon,
Annie

HEX MARKS THE SPOT

I spent most of my childhood at one of two tables. The first was our kitchen table, which was a built-in counter with four tall, wobbly stools. These were constructed by people who either didn't understand children or did understand them but just hated them. I liked to climb up on a stool, fall off of it, and then wail until someone comforted me (my mother) or until someone told me to shut up (my brother). Then, five minutes later, I'd do it all over again. I was slow to understand the cruel and strict headmaster we call gravity. There at my perch at the kitchen counter, my legs dangling high above the tile floor, I ruined many good times for my family. This is where I demanded fried rice and insisted that my mother—and only my mother—blow on all my food to cool it down. This is where I whined about being hungry and threw a tantrum when my snack didn't involve natural and/or artificial strawberries. This is where I announced celery would no longer be tolerated, even if it was slathered in (smooth) peanut butter, and where I rejected all cereals that were dangerously low in sugar. This is where I spilled juice, milk, soup, and everything else in the liquid state of matter and commanded someone else to clean up my mess. This is where I'd watch my mother cook four Korean dishes at once and then refuse to eat any of it because what I really wanted was a grilled cheese sandwich. I was a real asshole when I was four.

This is where my brother and I would protest every Saturday morning before going to Korean school and where we'd steal each other's Sunday-morning bacon before going to church. This is where I'd pick through my hashed browns to eat the diced Spam. For years, Spam was a regular part of our meals—a contribution from my dad's time working on a U.S. base in Seoul. Then one day my mother read the nutritional content and that was the sad and untimely end of a beautiful relationship.

The other table was in an open area near the kitchen. It was a hexagonal wood table with a wicker top covered by a hexagonal piece of glass. The wood chairs had matching wicker backs and thick seat cushions covered in nubby white fabric. The chairs were on casters, which wore away at the tan rug. This is where my brother and I did our homework—for regular school, Korean school, Bible school, and the extra worksheets our mother assigned to us. This is where I was lectured when I brought home a B+ in math and where I memorized multiplication tables with my mother. ("*Ayoo*, zero time one not one! How many time I tell you?") This is where my brother showed me how to draw a three-dimensional cube and blew my mind ("Whoa, it looks so real!"). It's also where he once—and only once—helped me with my math homework. ("Mom, she is unteachable. We should give up.") This was where I worked on my science fair project, and when I finally presented it at school, my teacher asked if I had any help from my father because I showcased a chemistry set with phenolphthalein and bromophenol blue, which are acid and base indictors;

industrial-grade pH testing strips; and a special machine that stirs solutions using magnets. I was in third grade.

This hexagonal table is where my parents sat and paid their bills and bickered over money. This is where my dad would read the *Korea Times,* which is published in Korean, while three days' worth of the *Los Angeles Times* piled up on our driveway. This is where my mom folded laundry and sewed buttons back onto clothes. It is where we threw down the groceries, the mail, and our backpacks and lunch boxes right when we walked in the door. When my mother had friends over for coffee, they sat around this table, leaned back in the wicker chairs, and complained about children, husbands, and produce. In that order, more or less.

Right after I finished sixth grade, our parents held a family meeting around this table and announced our move to a different suburb. My father's commute would be cut in half and we'd have access to better schools and, in addition, Koreans. We packed up the hexagon and ate one last meal at the old kitchen counter. In our new house, the hexagon became our new, old kitchen table.

This is where I declared vegetarianism, and where my mother snuck meat into my food ("Fish not real meat!"). This is where Mike and I got lectured about our SAT scores, speeding tickets, and casual attitudes toward curfew, washing dishes, and our futures. This is where I announced my retirement from piano lessons and Korean school, two things I still regret. When my parents brought home a copy of *U.S. News & World Report*'s college rankings, they sat around this table and encouraged me to apply to the top twenty-five schools, regardless of cost, location, or my desire to even go there. ("The Rose-Hulman Institute of Technology? Don't they run commercials during *Days of Our Lives*?") This is where my father outlined my mother's cancer treatment.

As we all aged, so did the hexagon. The wood became scuffed

and scraped, and the corners splintered. The glass was chipped in several places, and a layer of crumbs and filth had settled on the wicker underneath the glass that no amount of scrubbing could remove. The legs of the table were nicked from years and years of pushing in chairs with too much zest. The chairs themselves were in disrepair. The casters had become loose and some would buckle in the middle of meals. You could tell who sat where just by the impression our asses had made in the seats. It turns out that white is a poor color for kitchen chairs. You could track everything I ever ate just by analyzing the stains on the cushion, and discover new microorganisms in the process. After ten years, the table had survived plenty of action. After fifteen, it was battered and weary. After twenty-five years, the table was suffering a deep, relentless pain and needed to be euthanized. It was time for a new table where we could get into new arguments and make new memories, and time to leave the old behind. This opportunity came when my parents decided to downsize to a smaller home several years ago.

I returned from New York City to pack up my old bedroom. It was easy—I just threw everything out. Living in a tiny studio has taught me never to get attached to anything that has a length, width, or height. My brain might be cluttered with ideas, questions, and factoids about sea otters (the densest fur of any animal!), but I keep things disciplined and tidy in my quarters. When I buy new clothes, I donate old ones to make room. I recycle old electronics immediately, cash in loose change, and sell things I no longer want or need, like a blender—I don't like margaritas anymore; they taste like acid reflux. I do not collect CDs, DVDs, vinyl, ceramics, figurines, seashells, taxidermy, souvenir thimbles, or vintage nautical devices. I do not sew, knit, paint, scrapbook, or engage in any other hobby that requires needles, adhesives, or cups of water. I do not believe in sports that require balls, helmets, pads, specialized footwear, ropes, or swords. In contrast, my parents still have their rusted bikes with banana seats, broken skis, warped golf clubs, and old wood tennis rackets, which would be considered antiques now. In the garage, I found one of those machines with the belt you wrap around your midsection. When you turn it on, the belt jiggles violently and promotes what I assume is weight loss and an intense need to urinate. This is something they actually own. All of this garbage would end up on the walls of T.G.I. Friday's if only my parents could part with it. I knew that convincing my mother and father to throw away most of the crap that filled their home was going to be impossible. I had to pick my battles.

So, I picked the hexagon.

"Do you want me to drop off the table at Goodwill? I know a guy with a truck."

"Why we throw away table?" My father blinked at me. The expression on his face showed suspicion and confusion, with just a slight note of disregard.

The expression on my face also showed suspicion and confusion, but with a heavy note of are-you-fucking-kidding-me. "No, we're not throwing away the table. We're *donating*."

"Why we throw away table?"

"Because it's old? Look at it." I pointed to the faded edges of the table. The finish had been rubbed off in the spots where we rested our elbows and forearms. "We're basically the same age." I paused. "But only one looks good."

"Yes."

"Wait, I'm talking about myself. I'm the one that looks good, not the table. You got that, right?"

"Table is fine."

"What do you mean 'fine'? Have you ever noticed how sticky it is? No matter how much you clean it, the thing is always disgusting."

"We keep."

"Why? The chairs barely work."

"Chair work, Annie. If you can sit in it, then it work."

"No, when you sit in it, the casters fall off."

"What caster?"

"The wheels, you know, on the bottom." To demonstrate, I picked up a chair and tried to wrench off a caster.

"What you doing? Annie, stop!"

"I'm trying to make a point. The casters come off."

"No, no, I fix that long time ago. I superglue it."

During the Northridge earthquake, something fell on top of a toilet and broke the lid. Instead of buying a new seat, my father just taped the pieces back together. He didn't even use clear tape. He used black electrical tape. In addition, he taped a little geometric design onto the lid—diagonal lines and squares. He said he did it to disguise the repair with a decoration. For years, friends would come over and ask, "What is *up* with your toilet?"

"I fix all the chair. Table is good. It work."

"I know the table works. But that's not the point. It's gross."

"I repaint."

"You're going to repaint the table? With what?" I imagined my father using leftover house paint because he was too cheap to buy stain. Then I imagined toxic fumes coming off the table. I'd hallucinate and believe kleptomaniacs were stealing my thoughts and eventually pass out into my bowl of rice.

"What else? I paint with paint. Annie, this not concern you. This not your table."

In one corner of the glass top, there is a neat line of minuscule scratches. In first grade, Mike taught me that diamonds are the toughest things on Earth and that you could tell if a diamond was real if it could scratch glass. I took it upon myself to test all my mother's diamonds. Indeed, they were real. Later, I learned that lots of stuff scratches glass. Including cubic zirconia.

"Dad, it's ugly. Why not buy a new table? A nice one."

"This table fine. Why we throw away? New one is waste of money."

"Okay, how about this? *I'll* buy *you* a table. Oak, pine, some rare indigenous rainforest wood, whatever. And I'll even get you one with less than six sides. Maybe one with no sides." I gasped loudly and clapped my hands excitedly. "A circle, Dad! A circle!"

Korean dining involves picking at different side dishes, and on our kitchen table, the corners always stab me in the gut when I reach for *banchan*. I'm not sure why my parents bought a hexagon in the first place. Normal people eat off a circle or a rectangle, or perhaps even a square if they're feeling adventurous. But my parents are the type of deviants who like hexagons, which have just enough sides to be irritating but not enough to be interesting. Hexagons say, "Oh, you only have four sides? What a shame. I, of course, have six. It must be so hard for those poor triangles!" Hexagons flaunt their superiority, but deep down inside, they're just insecure little polygons that will never measure up to octagons.

"Annie, we keep."

"But I want to buy you a table. It would be my pleasure. An honor, really."

"This table fine."

"Plus, I'll buy you new chairs that *don't* smell. You'll get an entire set at a cost of zero United States dollars or zero South Korean won to you. *Gratis.* That means 'free' in Spanish."

"Annie. We keep everything. Go help you mommy."

On cue, my mother walked into the kitchen, arms filled with packing tape. "What?"

"Dad wants to keep this table. This old, putrid, and extremely ugly kitchen table."

"No."

"Yes."

"No!"

"Yes!"

"We get new one." My mother scowled and dropped a tape dispenser onto the hexagon in a clatter. She has a nice flair for drama, that one.

"This is not discussion. We keep."

"Why we keep *this*?" My mother gestured with a free hand at the table. I would've used a different hand gesture.

My father shook his head. "Not a choice. We take this table. We use it."

"I am prepared to buy you both a very excellent and high-quality kitchen table and spend an obscene amount of money on it. Maybe something made by the Amish—you know, built by people who *know* kitchen tables. The freaking Amish can rock it out, Dad."

"Anne, you mouth. Please."

"Mom, I said 'freaking.'"

"With what money?" My father waved me off. "You have no money, Annie."

"Dad, I have a job."

"Wait, our beautiful, intelligent, and one and only daughter wants to buy her parents a kitchen table? And you're telling her no?" My mother continued a volley in Korean. She loves getting free shit. Who doesn't?

"No, we take table."

"Mom, this table sucks."

"Mommy hate too."

"Holy fucking shit, *Dad,* are you going to take that fucking table?" My brother entered the kitchen and came into the fray. There were streaks of dust on his black shirt.

"You mouth, Mike!"

"Seriously, this table is a piece of shit."

"Mike!"

"I get splinters whenever I eat at this stupid fucking table."

"Mike!"

"Yeah, yeah, my mouth, whatever. You know how old this table is? It's fucking old, goddamn it. It's straight-up biblical."

My father tied off a garbage bag. "Everyone, this not a choice."

My brother pushed one of the chairs. "The casters are broken, too. You know that?"

"Actually, Mike, he superglued them." I smirked.

"Oh, what the fuck—what, Mom, *what*? Relax."

"We take table." My father stood in front of the hexagon, as if to shield it from us bloodthirsty savages. "Mike can help move it."

"What if Mike, like, accidentally dropped it?" I shrugged innocently.

My mother started laughing. My father did not.

"I hate this table." I rolled my eyes.

"Mommy hate table."

"I fucking can't stand this fucking table. Yes, everyone calm the fuck down about my mouth."

"Your mouth doesn't bother me, Mike."

"Thank you, Annie."

"This is not election."

"What?" My brother looked at me expectantly, silently asking for a translation. I couldn't help.

"There is no vote." Our father folded his arms across his chest.

"No one would vote for this table. It'd be like the Walter fucking Mondale of kitchen tables."

We all stared blankly.

"Hello? He ran against Reagan? Only won two states? Anyone?"

"Dad, I want to *buy* you a table just so I never, ever have to look at this one again."

"Sometime, it tear my sweater." My mother shook her head sadly. She pointed to the splintering wicker on the back of her chair. "My cashmere."

"No more discussion." My father handed me an empty box. "Help Mommy pack kitchen."

So, that was it. They moved it. The hexagon made it (safely) onto the truck and found its way into their new home.

When I visit, this is where my mother serves me sliced persimmons with little toothpicks in them. This is where we trim bean sprouts together while she tells me about all the extremely handsome, extremely successful, and extremely available sons of her church friends. This is where she watches me eat and gives me a rundown of her favorite Korean dramas, and then eats whatever I've left over. This is where I leave the random items my mother asks me to get for her—a container for soy sauce that's "not too big or small," a computer mouse, potpourri. This is where my father sat in his electric-blue Snuggie and read the driver's manual of his new car from cover to cover—several times—and asked my mother to do the same when she got her new car. Which she did not.

• • •

When my parents first moved to the States, a neighbor in their apartment building invited them over for Thanksgiving dinner. Eventually my mother decided to adopt the holiday even though she didn't particularly care about the Pilgrims, or, for that matter, turkey. There are no turkeys on the Korean peninsula. My mother can cook pork, fish, or beef in over a hundred different ways, but with turkey, she can only cook it one way: dry and bland. At least that's what I remember, anyway. I actually turned vegetarian on Thanksgiving. I woke up on a Thursday morning in 1992 to the sound of my mother overwhipping mashed potatoes with a mixer and decided, yes, today is the day.

Two years ago, my brother decided to roast a turkey for Thanksgiving. He researched recipes, read food blogs, and watched a bunch of cooking videos. Mike was really committed to it. I never go home for Thanksgiving; the travel is sadistic, both financially and emotionally.

"He spend almost one hundred on turkey! Most expensive turkey Mommy ever see," my mother sputtered into the phone.

"Wait, the turkey itself cost a hundred dollars? Was it wearing jewelry?"

"*Ayoo,* one hundred! *Behk bul!* All the wine and spice, so expensive. Pilgrim must be very rich."

"I'm sure it'll taste like a million bucks."

My brother is a lot like my father in that he follows written directions step-by-step. One reason why my father's old car lasted over twenty years (and over three hundred thousand miles) is because of his strict adherence to the car manual. My mother and I are the opposite. We tend to disregard manuals and recipes and just wing it, and then at some point the engine catches on fire and the biscotti tastes like grout.

The day after Thanksgiving, I called my brother to hear about his one-hundred-dollar turkey. Mike explained that he had baked it for two and a half hours, until the meat thermometer reached exactly 161 degrees Fahrenheit, not one degree more or less. He let the bird rest on the counter and reveled in all the compliments from my mother: "Oh my gosh, look at turkey, this you can order at Velvet Turtle!" Then he moved the turkey to the hexagon so he could ceremoniously carve up the bird, just like our Korean ancestors did when they shared a meal with Squanto and the rest of the Wampanoag people.

And then the hexagon shattered.

Glass cracked and exploded underneath the hot pan, and shards of glass rained onto the floor. The tray busted through the glass top and landed on the wicker surface with a loud thump. Everyone screamed.

"Holy mother of shit. Oh. My. God. Mike," I gasped into the phone.

"I fucked up, I know, I know."

"Why didn't you put down a hot pad?"

"It had been out of the oven for a while. I thought it'd be fine."

"Everyone uses a hot pad! It's what civilized people do."

"A hot pad wouldn't have done jack shit anyway." Turns out, the temperature of the bird rises five to ten degrees after it's taken out of the oven. "You know, Mom always puts hot shit onto the table."

"She uses a hot pad! Also, a pan of fish is different from a gigantic turkey you bake at six hundred degrees."

"It's three fifty degrees and, dude, I already heard all this. I don't need to hear this from you, you fucking vegetarian."

I hung up and immediately called my mother to get more details. Apparently my father had stood there silently, lips pursed, while she yelled at everyone to get away from the glass and sprang into action with the broom. I wish I had been there to see the

death of the hexagon. I would've dragged its remains to the backyard and set them on fire.

"But you know what? Best turkey Mommy ever taste. I can't
believe. So juice."

"I'll still buy you a new kitchen table. I can order it online. I
don't think the Amish have a website though."

"Anne . . . Daddy want to keep table."

"WHAT? No. No."

"Yes. We have to keep it." She sounded resigned. She is not a
woman who gives up. She pushed us to get straight A's, pushed me
through three musical instruments, and pushed through cancer.
But even she couldn't win against the hexagon.

"But the table has no glass. So, you're just putting stuff on the
wicker? I can't stand wicker. It's so hard to clean and it's not durable." At that moment, I realized something important: I'm the
type of person who has strong opinions about wicker.

"We eat at dining room now." The dining room was never,
ever used. It should have been cleared for something more useful,
like a bounce house.

"Why are you keeping the table if you're not even using it?"

"Mommy don't know and Mommy don't care."

I got off the phone and called my brother. "Here's the plan: I'll
order a table right now. When it gets delivered, throw the old one
away. Take it to West Covina or something. Dad will never find
it there."

"Dude, West Covina's an hour away."

"Whatever. He won't say shit because the new table will be so
fucking amazing. And also round."

"He'd go ballistic."

"Sure, he'll be angry, but he'll also be the owner of a badass
kitchen table. Again, to be clear, it'll be round."

"I don't want any part of this. I've pissed him off enough. Dad obviously has some kind of emo attachment to that piece of shit."

"No one ever lets me do anything in this family."

A week later, my brother called me with horrible news. "Dad's going to get new glass for the table."

"Oh, really? From where? Discount Glass Hexagon Emporium?"

"He says he knows a guy."

"He 'knows a guy'? Someone who can make a glass hexagon? That's impossible."

"I don't know, a guy in Burbank."

"A piece of custom glass is going to cost more than a new kitchen table. He's on dust."

"And he's not sharing."

A few months later, I visited my parents. I expected to see the old table outfitted with a new piece of glass—and that's exactly what I saw. But there was something different about the table. The chairs were the same ones we'd had for the last thirty years, but something else was off.

The top was not a hexagon. It was square.

A massive piece of square glass was sitting on top of the table. About four inches of glass were hanging over the sides of the hexagon.

"*Mom!* What is this?"

She shook her head. "You daddy buy glass."

"Yes."

"But glass not fit."

"Yes, because the glass is a square. And the table is not."

"He say he cut glass. Do it himself." She closed her eyes, her head hung low, her spirit crushed. Had I not been so outraged, I might've wept.

"*Dad* is going to cut the glass? With what? You need special tools. You can't use scissors." I called my brother immediately. "I thought you said Dad knew a guy who could make a glass hexagon?"

"Turns out he just knew a guy with glass."

"You've got to be kidding me."

"At first he wanted to go to a place that specialized in windshields, but I told him no."

I imagined myself eating on a windshield. After I finished, I could turn on the wipers to clean off the mess. Maybe spray some soap too. At least it'd be safety glass and wouldn't shatter. "Did Dad measure the table first? Or did he just walk in and say, 'I'd like some glass, please'?"

"He just eyeballed it."

"Did his eyeballs not realize the table is a *hexagon*?"

"A custom job was going to be too expensive."

"Told you so! Told you so! I'm going to get rid of it."

"Annie, no. It's not worth it."

"Yes, it is."

"You have to let him have his way."

"But his way sucks."

"Dude, it's not even your table."

I hung up the phone. I sat down to my favorite lunch, rice noodles with sesame oil, tofu, cucumbers, and kimchi. My mother sat down to my left—as far as I can remember, she has always sat to my left—and picked at my food, insisting that she wasn't hungry enough to get her own plate. As I reached for different dishes, the glass wobbled underneath.

My mother secured the glass top with her hands. "Maybe I use tablecloth so it stop shake."

"That's like putting a Band-Aid on a broken leg. It's not going to help."

Our table had endured decades of abuse, both physical and emotional. Every major gouge, scrape, and scar had a story, but there were so many no one could remember them all. Was this nick from when Mike dropped his pocketknife or was it from when my grandmother dropped a tray of *galbi*? Was this stain from when my mother broke a bottle of nail polish or was it from the kachina doll I painted for a fourth-grade art project? The hexagon had witnessed our family's jokes, arguments, and tears. It had persevered through floods of soup, juice, and pork grease. It had made it through a 6.7 earthquake unscathed and only narrowly survived a Thanksgiving turkey. The table was here to stay—a part of our family—and would stick around for another thirty years of my mother's *yook gae jang*, my father's car manuals, my brother's foul mouth, and my indignant outrage.

I grumbled.

"What can you do, Anne?"

"Nothing."

Hi, Sandwich,

Did you know that the average American eats about two hundred sandwiches a year? Two hundred! That's a two followed by two zeros! That's roughly four sandwiches per week. That means four times a week, average Americans have this conversation:

"What do you want for lunch?"

"I don't know, what do you want?"

"I don't know, I asked you first."

"I don't know. Screw it, let's just get a sandwich."

"Fine, but I ate that yesterday."

"*Everyone* ate that yesterday."

You are the default lunch. You are what people eat when they don't have time or don't have a better option or don't feel like eating pizza for some mysterious and stupid reason. You are what people eat when they can't bother with forks or with those one-dimensional utensils called spoons. You are uninspiring. You are two pieces of bread with stuff in between them, but somehow you're not a hamburger and you're not as cute as toast. Even if you get dolled up with cured meats or exotic cheeses, or get sassy with heirloom microvegetables from a local, woman-owned, wind-powered farm, you still get lost among the other 199 unremarkable sandwiches of the year. Remember the one at the airport? Or the one from the cafeteria? No? Well, it had too many onions. Fact: Onion on a sandwich is the culinary equivalent of a wedgie. You have to pick it out and sometimes you have to fish for it.

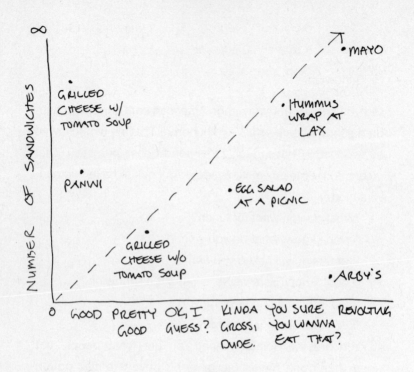

DISAPPOINTMENT

Sometimes people eat breakfast for dinner. Restaurants will serve breakfast twenty-four hours a day so people can enjoy an exhilarating and satisfying meal that breaks convention. You can see it on their happy faces as they eat: "It's eight o'clock at night, motherfuckers, look at my giant stack of pancakes!" But there's not a single restaurant that exclaims, "Lunch served all day!" That's because lunch means sandwiches, and no one wants to eat a sandwich for dinner. It's a fact. I know because I've asked everyone in the United States, which is where most average Americans live. The response is always the same: I'd rather eat cereal, and actually, I did last night.

Listen, I like you, in general. You fill a need. You provide a service, one where you enter my stomach when it's empty. But on most days, you make me sad, especially when I'm on my 105th sandwich of the fiscal year. You convince me that eating is a chore, a soulless but necessary task, like plunging a toilet—something you wouldn't have to do if you didn't eat. You make me want food pellets, like what rabbits and chinchillas eat. The pellets make them so happy. I wish to be that happy. Meaning that I wish to eat kibble of dried alfalfa and maize instead of you, a sandwich. But I read that food pellets are impossible for humans because to get enough nutrition and fiber, the pellet would have to be the size of a softball. Which, ironically, is the size of a sandwich if you squish it up into a ball. This is actually something I did to my ham sandwiches in elementary school. Even at eight years of age, I knew that you, sandwich, were bullshit.

I know I have a first-world luxury of complaining about food. I am a lucky sandwich-eating person. But I am also an unlucky sandwich-eating person. You are the food manifestation of "It is what it is," which is one of the least inspirational things you can say to someone. It means, "Hey, there's nothing you can do about this today or tomorrow or ever, so why don't you sit down and decide whether you want wheat or white?" So yes, sandwich, "it is what it is." I'll see you tomorrow at lunch.

Best,
Annie

MIDAS TOUCH

Last year, my father ate a sandwich. Roast beef. It was a very special sandwich. Momentous. Historic even. It taught him an important lesson about the fragility of life, the importance of family, and all that other garbage. The sandwich came with everything— lettuce, tomato, pickles, mustard, and a colony of bacteria that puréed his insides. Actually, it was less like a colony and more like an advanced civilization, one with robot armies. Nothing would stay down. My father was moaning and whimpering and sweating and flushing, ruing roast beef and the world in general. My mother tried to get him to see a doctor, but he couldn't be more than two feet from a bathroom. He insisted that it would pass, and it did, two days later. I happened to be visiting on vacation. My father was recovering in bed, sipping roasted-corn tea, which tastes exactly how it sounds: delicious.

"I should've gone to Arby."

"You would've had the same problem at Arby's. Maybe worse."

"Nothing can be worse."

"Things can always be worse. Mom taught me that."

"Daddy very sick, Annie." He adjusted a pillow behind his head.

"You said you were feeling better."

"I am, but I was very, very sick." He put his hand on his belly. "I think I almost die."

"Oh, come on." I snorted, a little too loudly.

"I think what happen to our family if I die?"

"It was just food poisoning. You act like you've never had it before."

"Never like this."

"It happens to everyone. I got it last year." Also from a sandwich—a soy-meatball hero. It was no hero. "You feel like you're never going to eat again, but then it goes away and you eat all the same crap you ate before and life is awesome. You know what? I ate from a truck yesterday."

"Truck?"

"Yeah, a taco truck."

"How come you eat from truck? You have no money?" My father frowned.

"No, Dad, you're missing the point. I ate from a truck. It had no running water. And it was excellent. Five stars, whatever. I'm still alive."

"No, this different. I almost die, Annie." He shook his head gravely.

"You weren't even close to dying." He was more like living inconveniently for a short period of time.

"I think what would Mommy do? She be in trouble, big trouble."

"No, she'd be annoyed. Planning a funeral is a pain in the ass." I grimaced. "So I hear."

"I realize I need to prepare."

"For what?"

"For when I'm gone."

"Drama queen." I rolled my eyes.

"I won't live forever."

"Sure, but you're not going to die tomorrow. Unless I kill you."

"You never know. Tomorrow I'm meeting lawyer for my will."

"Are you kidding me?"

"Why I joke? We have to plan for future, Annie."

"Dad. You. Ate. A sandwich."

The following week, my father asked me to come to his lab to discuss his imminent death, among other things. He prefers to talk about serious business in his lab because that's where he does serious business. When people think of labs, they usually picture antiseptic, organized workspaces with beakers and Bunsen burners. Lots of pipettes. They imagine scientists in spotless white coats and protective eyewear, looking through a microscope, studying stem cells or a cure for cancer or a rare strain of anthrax. Maybe some combination of the three. Whatever the case, the working environment is clean and well lit, essential for doing science stuff. My father's lab does not look like this. He doesn't even have a white coat. He actually did have one, but when I was in fifth grade I borrowed it for a Korean school skit about a deranged doctor who chases a patient with a giant syringe. It was the closest I've ever gotten to becoming a doctor. After, I used the coat as a robe. I have no idea where it went.

My father's lab is more like a garage, one with graduated cylinders. Everything is covered with a thick layer of grime. Shelves are packed with chemistry reference books and manuals for every single machine in his office, from the fume hood to the fax machine. Wire baskets and trays are filled with papers, all yellow and brittle with age. The counters are littered with soiled notepads, dirty beakers and Erlenmeyer flasks, glass stir-rers, rusty tongs, bent paper clips, and pens with no caps. There are jugs and bottles of chemicals that I assume cause death, dis-memberment, or something in between (which is actually worse than either death or dismemberment), and there are large bins caked with a substance that looks like Frosted Flakes. Scattered throughout the lab are cups of chemicals and mugs of Sanka—neither of which you should drink. The concrete floor, which hasn't been mopped since 1991, is stained, scuffed, chipped, gouged, and cracked. The walls are dingy, and the lighting is fluorescent and unflattering. It makes everything in the room look jaundiced, including the people. There are refrigerator-sized machines, whose functions I will never understand, and there's also a refrigerator, whose function I do understand: to hold food years beyond its expiration date. The bathroom is not something anyone should see, use, or even discuss. There's a filthy bar of soap in there, which is confusing because soap seems like something that would clean itself.

The lab is tucked away behind a strip mall, which was once the site of a major defense plant. When the facility shut down in the nineties, my father helped himself to discarded bookcases, desks, chairs, and even phones. The furniture was from the seven-ties and eighties and already in various states of disrepair. Today it's on the brink of disintegration, barely existing in space-time. The swivel chairs are lumpy and ripped, with foam and springs bursting from the cushions, and the armrests are patched up with duct tape. The desks are well worn and lopsided—not that you can tell underneath the mounds of detritus. My father arranged four large desks in the middle of his lab so they'd look like a grand conference table, except the desks are different widths, heights, colors, and styles. It's the furniture equivalent of a ransom note.

Imagine the drawer in your house that's filled with miscellaneous crap—every home has one. It's where you keep a growing collection of rubber bands and spare keys to some forgotten place or vehicle. Each of my father's four desks has about four drawers. If you do the math, four times four is equal to one thousand, so there are one thousand crap drawers in his "conference table." If you open each one—which is challenging because the drawers stick—you'll discover everything from broken magnifying glasses to stamps, which would be considered collector's items if they were in better condition. There are rolls of thirty-two-cent stamps in there. The last time it cost thirty-two cents to mail a letter, people were stockpiling canned goods for Y2K. Fact: People ate a lot of chili in 2000.

My father started his lab over twenty years ago, a one-man operation, until recently. He works about 6.5 days a week, leaving the house well before rush hour and coming home well after. From what I can understand, companies give him a sample, and he tells them what's in it—specifically, the amount of gold. When the defense industry was actually an industry in California, he'd get a box of circuit boards, bits of machinery, or other random scraps where gold is used as a conductor. They were discarded or unused parts from a variety of machines; I like to think they came from lasers, either the ones that cut metal or the ones that destroy aliens. My father would figure out how much gold was in them, and the company would determine if it was cost-effective to strip it off or just dump it into the ocean like everything else. After the defense industry waned, he began working with jewelry companies. He assayed the amount of gold in by-products generated from the manufacturing or polishing of jewelry. He also gold-plated sample pieces for them. I don't fully understand the process, but I know it involves flesh-eating acids and electricity.

Also, science. My father's work serves a market that is so niche that I'm surprised he's stayed in business all these years.

I arrived at the lab as my father was working on an assay. He was measuring something on a scale, squinting at the display even though he was wearing glasses. He was wearing his lab clothes— ragged pants and a faded shirt with holes caused by acid splatters. My father doesn't bother with aprons, gloves, or goggles. Or safety. His hands and arms are scarred from cuts and burns; you can see the history of his work as a chemist. In high school, I had a science teacher who'd walk around the classroom and oversee our experiments. If he didn't like something, he'd call out, "Bad technique!" and remind us about a student who literally burned his eyes off. Mr. Walker would probably go hoarse in my father's lab.

My father directed me to a chair. "Sit, Annie."

I cringed. "It's dirty."

"What you mean? It's clean."

"Says who?"

"I clean it just for you."

I scowled. "I'm wearing my nice jeans."

He shook his head and gave me a roll of paper towels, which were smudged with dark fingerprints. I tore a few sheets off and sat on top of them.

"This is just like the bathroom in the Port Authority."

"It not that bad." My father took a seat across from me. Then he stood up and swapped chairs. "This one uncomfortable."

"They're all uncomfortable." I moved around in my seat, trying to settle in. The paper towels got stuck on a piece of duct tape.

"One day I'm going to die."

"Jesus Christ, Dad."

"I talk to lawyer, everything set."

"What does that mean? Did you buy a coffin?"

"No."

"Okay, then. Everything is *not* set." I started to lean back in my chair and then stopped myself because the backrest was grungy.

"I want cremation."

"Fine. Where do you want us to spread your ashes?"

"I don't know."

"See? You haven't thought this through." I sighed. "Whatever."

"Do you want the house?"

"No."

"Why not, it's nice!"

"What am I going to do with it?"

"Live in it, what else you do with house?"

When my parents downsized, they moved to a suburb forty miles outside L.A. The neighborhood is charmless; it's a tract-housing development. The house has carpet, which I find hyper-allergenic, and there's no real backyard, which totally defeats the purpose of living in Southern California. I think houses in L.A. don't even need roofs. Just really big umbrellas.

"I don't want the house. I live in New York. Give it to Mike."

"Mike doesn't want it."

"Fine, then we'll sell it." I shrugged. "But definitely leave him your car." My brother bought his car on Craigslist for a great price, but the trunk is stuck and doesn't open. There's either a dead hooker or a suitcase of cash in there. "What else?"

"Annie. Future is very serious."

"Sure, but you have, like, twenty more years to figure this all out."

"Maybe only two year."

"Dad, it was *just* a roast beef sandwich."

"I want to retire." My father was about to celebrate his seventieth birthday.

"So do it. Why are you waiting, especially if you're going to die next month?"

"Business bad right now so I have to wait."

"Do you have a retirement plan?"

"No."

"Not even a 401(k)?"

"No."

"So, can you and Mom manage on Social Security?" This conversation was turning into a commercial: a silver-haired, road-weary man sitting at a table with a young financial consultant—"Your future, our goals." Of course, I'm in no position to advise on anyone's finances. I'm still paying off loans and recently my bank sent a notice that they were freezing my savings account due to "prolonged inactivity."

"Don't worry, Annie, I have plan." He yanked open a drawer and brought out a canvas bag. The name of a bank was stamped on the side.

"Dad, are you saving your money in a bag?" Koreans, in general, mistrust banks and prefer to deal in cash. A few years ago, my mom and I bought plane tickets to Seoul from a Korean travel agent. I had over thirteen hundred dollars in my purse, much of it in tens and twenties. I felt like a drug dealer, paranoid and looking over my shoulder every two seconds. My mother thought a thick stack of bills was no big deal. I imagine this is how Bill Gates feels. I read that if he dropped a thousand dollars on the floor, it wouldn't be worth his time to pick it up. In the two seconds he'd waste by tugging up his khakis and bending over, he could've made a decision worth much, much more than that. I read about it on the Internet so I know it's true.

"No, no, not like that. This just a bag. No cash." He fumbled with the zipper and showed me the contents.

I stared. Ogled. Gawked. Eyes wide, mouth agape.

There were five bars of gold.

As in, gold ingots. Gold bullion. Bars. Made out of gold. Fucking gold.

"HOLY SHIT, IS THAT REAL?"

"Of course it real."

"OH MY GOD."

The bars were small, not the giant bricks you see in the movies. Nonetheless, they were still bars of fucking gold. The color was dazzling.

"Dad, where did you get these?"

"I bought." He shrugged.

"From where? Bars-of-gold-dot-net? Who sells these?" I picked one up. It was heavier than it looked, it being fucking gold and all.

"Company buy gold all the time. How you think they make gold necklace? Or gold parts for electronic? Some people buy gold just to have."

"Just to have for what? You can't go to the grocery store and pay with this." I imagined a Hawaiian-shirt-clad cashier at Trader Joe's, calling the manager over: *This gentleman would like to buy the chipotle hummus with this bullion.*

"I use it for work, when I gold-plate. Sometimes I buy gold when it cheap and then I sell when it goes up. Gold is high right now. So I'm going to sell. Then, I retire."

I realized that this was how my father had gotten through the collapse of the defense industry and all the recessions. No matter what state the economy is in, gold is always valuable. It's kind of like how plumbers are never out of a job. Everybody poops. "And you just keep them in a drawer? What's wrong with you?" I looked around us to make sure no one was going to bust in and steal my father's bars of fucking gold.

"No one even see my lab. It look like nothing from outside."

"If it's stolen, you're out, like, a squillion dollars."

"It not worth *that* much."

"How much is it worth?"

"You don't have to worry about that."

"Tell me! How much?"

My father shooed me away. "Mommy and I will be okay. I plan for our future." He put the bag back in the desk.

"You don't want to put it in a safe? That drawer doesn't even lock."

"Annie, it's not big deal."

"Are you insane? You're keeping gold in a drawer. You know what belongs in a drawer? Pants."

My father sighed. So did I. We were two grossly misunderstood people, each on our own islands of common sense.

"I'm going to sell." He scanned my neck, wrists, and fingers. "You want me to gold-plate anything?"

"No, but thanks."

"Not even you earring?"

"My earrings are fine."

"But they silver. Don't you want gold?"

"No, I'm good."

"But gold earring would be nice."

"Seriously, Dad. Let it go."

Back when my father worked for the large petroleum-production company, part of his duties included gold-plating components—not sure what exactly, but I'm sure they were used to drill, mine, and kill adorable animals and their innocent, dewy-eyed babies. The company's lab, which I visited once, was actually the kind people imagine. It was sterile and organized. There was an eyewash station and several fire extinguishers in case someone caught on fire. My father even had a hard hat with his name on it. Gold-plating was—and is—my father's favorite task. I can see why—you take something kind of boring, like a piece of wire, and then you turn it into something useful and valuable. Beautiful, even. Gold is dense, malleable, and a good conductor. It dissipates heat and doesn't corrode or oxidize in air and water. Pretty much every electronic device, from cell phones to satellites, uses gold. It's used in glass, astronauts' helmets, cancer treatments, Gold-schläger, and trophies awarded to the world's greatest boss. Plus, it looks nice around your neck.

After a few years on the job, my father gold-plated an old ring for my mother, something she'd had for years and never wore. It went from a dingy silver to a brilliant gold.

"Wow! It looks real!"

"It *is* real. Twenty-four karat."

Thus began my father's Gold Rush. He started plating my mother's silver pieces. An old necklace became worthy of wear. An unassuming cuff turned into a statement piece. A tarnished brooch laid to rest at the bottom of a jewelry box was transformed into a festive piece that really tied an outfit together. Once my father disassembled a bracelet, gold-plated each bead, and put it back together again. Kind of. He sat at the kitchen table, frustrated and cross-eyed, trying to pull a thin thread through the tiny baubles. I ended up finishing the project for him. I was in fourth grade and my fingers were small and nimble like those of the sweatshop worker who probably made the bracelet in the first place. My father thanked me with a gold-plated pin. Which I lost two days later.

Eventually my father finished my mother's silver jewelry, but his gold bug remained. So he began gold-plating her gold-plated jewelry. In other words, he made things that were already gold even more gold. Dull gold chains would come back a deeper, shinier gold. Lighter pieces would come back darker. If my father was unsatisfied with the luster of a gold pendant, he'd strip and replate it. A piece that was eighteen karat became twenty-four karat. He kept a reference guide around for my mother. It's kind of like a book of fabric swatches, except with plated bars that range from white gold to a gaudy shade only Leprechauns would love. Eventually he turned all of my mother's jewelry into glimmering pieces of gold, with the exception of the ones that were actually solid gold. People would compliment her earrings and ask, "Oh are those new?" and she'd just smile and say, "Maybe." She gave off an air of status, even if the status was gold-plated.

Soon, my father moved on to my jewelry. I didn't have much. I was young and didn't care for it. My favorite piece was a plush dog whose tail wrapped around my wrist. My father couldn't have plated that even if he wanted to. Most of my necklaces were plastic, the beads cracked and chipped from being chewed. But my father did gold-plate a few items for me. A two-dollar pendant of a unicorn now looked like it was worth two dollars and fifty-three cents. When I was eight, my aunt gave me a tiny gold locket—the same one my cousin Tina had, so we could match. The next morning, while I was still sleeping, my father took it out of my jewelry box, a flowery case with a red satin lining and a ballerina that spun around. Tina had the same one, too. My father plated the locket and chain a radiant gold and missed the entire point and poetry of having matching necklaces. I was disappointed, but a minute later I forgot all about it.

In third grade, I began playing with my mother's jewelry, putting on every single chain, ring, and bracelet and parading around the house. I looked somewhere between Elizabeth Taylor and Mr. T. Then I'd put everything back exactly the way I found it before my mother got home from work. Once my grandmother caught me playing with the jewelry and the following week, she got me a necklace. It had an Italian good luck charm, designed to ward off the evil eye. My grandmother had no idea what it was; she just liked the shape. It was a tiny wavy horn that, when I look at it now, reminds me of a sperm. It was silver when I first got it and gold by the time I put it on.

My father, who had now effectively gold-plated all our jewelry, including his own watchband, set his eyes elsewhere. Particularly, on a pair of ducks—not real ducks, just little statues. Traditionally, duck figurines are given as wedding gifts. They symbolize a long and happy marriage; ducks mate for life. (They actually don't, but that is neither here nor there.) The ducks had been in our living room for as long as I could remember and provided an entertaining mode of transport for my dolls, especially since Mike wouldn't let me play with his RC jeep. ("You're a bad driver.") My father scooped the ducks off the coffee table and a week later, they returned as flashing beacons of gold.

"Don't they look nice, Annie?"

"I thought they looked nice before."

"They were brass." My father cringed.

"What's wrong with brass?"

"No one like brass." My father stepped back from the coffee table to admire his work. "Much better now."

"They're just ducks." I moved one around and left fingerprints, which my dad wiped off immediately.

He scanned the mantel. "I'm going to do candlestick too."

"Why? We never use them."

"We'll use more if they gold."

A week later we had two shimmering candlesticks. Which we've used exactly once, after the earthquake. He continued to gold-plate a few more knickknacks around the house—paperweights, commemorative coins, small statuettes. Our house could easily have turned into King Tut's tomb, but my father got busy at work.

At some point, I realized gold was for moms. In other words, old ladies. I could see it on the mothers at Korean school, the callous soul who was a piano teacher, the First Lady, and the cast of *Dallas,* a show I didn't like. I couldn't have cared less about rich people and their problems—I had my own, thank you. In sixth grade, the preppy girls, the punk girls, and everyone in between were dripping in silver, from headbands to toe rings. Silver was for the hip and trendy. I was neither of these things. I was an eighty-year-old senior with gout, putting on her best to shuffle down to the rec room for the Sunny Horizons Craft Jamboree. I shunned my gold and bought a slap bracelet, which my mother said made me look homeless. As if that's a thing homeless people wear.

Then my friend gave me a necklace for my birthday. It had a small plastic heart with a red rose and a sequin that was supposed to be a diamond. The chain was silver. Beautiful, chic, age-appropriate silver. I squealed and said it was, like, the best thing I'd ever gotten in my whole life, and I meant it. I wore it home.

"Is that new necklace, Annie?" My father eyed it. "Can I see?"

My father inspected the thickness of the chain and the quality of the clasp. He pulled it gently between his fingers, examining the links. The necklace was probably from Thrifty Drugs, but by the way my father appraised it, you'd think it was from Harry Winston.

"Claudia gave it to me."

"I can make better."

"But there's nothing wrong with it."

"I can make gold. I can do eighteen karat."

"I like silver."

"Anne, why have silver when you can have gold?"

"Why have gold when you can have silver?"

"Because gold better."

"Says who?"

"Says everyone. Gold worth more than silver."

"I don't care. This necklace is silver. I want to keep it that way."

"Annie, it not real silver. Not sterling." My father examined it more closely. "Probably nickel."

"I don't care. If you touch this, I'm gonna go off."

"Off?"

"Like, go *off*. Go crazy."

"Anne, you daddy not crazy." My mother glared at me. "*Ayoo, so rude.*"

"That's not what I said," I scoffed. "Mom, he wants to change my necklace."

"Let him change, gold is nice."

"If Claudia wanted to give me a gold necklace, then she would've given me one, duh."

My father shook his head. "I think she be happier if I make it gold."

"Dad, you don't even know her."

"She's the girl from El Salvador," my mother explained in Korean. "Lives down the street. Big, curly hair."

"Oh, she's nice girl. She would like you to have gold necklace."

I snatched the chain and ran up to my room, where I hid it from King Midas and his gold-plated touch. Every morning, I put it on after I arrived at school, the way some girls put in their nose rings.

Then in seventh grade, it was stolen out of my gym locker. I was crushed. A symbol of my friendship and of my determination, gone.

My father can cook exactly two things. The first is Rice Krispies treats, though they are far from treats. They are crispy, however. Very, very crispy. The second is "steakie." He takes two cuts of London broil and dusts each side with salt, pepper, garlic powder, and MSG, which is as magical as it is maligned. I'm not sure how he came up with this recipe. It's certainly not Korean. Koreans take beef very seriously; Texans aren't the only ones known for barbecue. My mother would rather die than use garlic powder, but just for my father, she stocks the kitchen with a large container. It looks like a tub of sand. Whenever we ate steakie, my father would use scissors to cut the meat into bite-sized cubes because our old knives couldn't cut through the overcooked slabs. When I was in ninth grade, my mother bought a fancy set of steak knives. They came in an embroidered silk sleeve, with padded pockets and ties that secured each knife in place. The blades were deadly enough to destroy a hunk of my father's beef. The handles were understated—slim, but rounded and heavy. And silver.

"Very good quality." My father nodded, actually satisfied with my mother's selection. He usually thinks everything she buys is unnecessary, overpriced, or both. As a result, my mother's good at returning or hiding her purchases. She's also good at sneaking in new items as if they've been there all along. ("I've had this sweater forever, how do you not remember seeing it?") My father rummaged in our crap drawer and brought out his gold-plating reference guide. "How about this color?" He pointed to a deep orange-gold.

"Dad, are you going to gold-plate the knives?"

"Yes." He flipped a page in his guide. "Maybe lighter better?"

"Seriously? Why would you do that?"

"Why not?"

"We can't be eating with gold knives, Dad. That's tacky."

"Gold nice. How many times I have to tell you?"

"There's a fine line between classy and tacky." My friend's mother had a silver tea-service set. The teapot, tray, creamer, and sugar bowl were stamped with a gorgeous, ornate arabesque pattern. But every single piece was covered in plastic wrap so it wouldn't tarnish. She had even individually wrapped the tiny spoons. The set was displayed on a mirrored liquor cart, with silver handles that were also plastic-wrapped. So something classy was turned horrifically tacky. "Gold knives? Don't you think that's a little much?"

"I'll make them look good."

"Just because it looks good to you doesn't mean it actually looks good."

One of my favorite shows is *MTV Cribs,* which showcases the homes of celebrities with obscene amounts of money and very little taste. I love watching hip-hop moguls tout their $100,000 Gucci sheets or their custom rides with Louis Vuitton airbags. Most of these rappers, pop stars, and athletes came from nothing, and now they have way too much. It's a sick and fascinating display of status. But the real reason why I love the show—diamond-crusted stripper poles aside—is seeing how their belongings reflect their values and idiosyncrasies. One producer pointed out his marble floors—they were expensive, imported from a small village in Italy, and, most important, kept his feet cool in the summer. A singer had a two-story closet filled with her designer shoes, all organized by color and style, each in a clear plastic box labeled with a Polaroid. But out of everything I've seen, my favorite is Russell Simmons's gilded bathroom, which features gold-leaf walls and floor, a gold vanity, a gold trash can, and a gold toilet paper dispenser (no, the toilet paper is not gold). The crown jewel, however, is the deluxe gold toilet. It's quite the throne. I don't know what this says about Russell Simmons's values or idiosyncrasies, but I do know that the stuff that comes out of his ass is treated better than the rest of the world. If my father were more of a baller, he'd install a gold toilet in every bathroom. What we have instead is a souvenir plate from Korea. It pictures a traditional house with a thatch roof and the name of some fishing town. There's a band of gold around the edge and a label that says "24k." It's not a small label. Why my father chose to buy a gold-plated plate when he could plate one himself, I'm not sure. Maybe it was a moment of weakness at the gift shop and he just couldn't resist the pull of twenty-four glorious karats. I find it tacky, but my father loves it. It's on display next to a gold-plated crucifix.

"Dad, gold knives will look trashy. What would guests think?"

"They think we have nice knife."

"No, they'd think we were trying to act rich."

"We rich, Annie."

"No, we're comfortable, and rich people don't have gold knives. You know who does? Pirates." I covered an eye. "Arr, where's me gold?"

My father ignored me and flipped another page in his reference guide. "I think this color best."

"Maybe you can just do the handles? Please?"

A week later he brought home the knives. He had only plated the handles—not because of my suggestion, but because the gold finish on the blades would've worn off over time and that would've "look cheap." I was relieved. And impressed. The handles glowed a muted yellow-orange. The contrasting silver blade put a twist on an otherwise banal object. The knives weren't as garish as I thought they'd be. They were kind of tasteful, really. Then I stopped and slapped some reality into myself. My father had covered our knives in gold. Fucking gold. It was ridiculous. My friends' fathers coached soccer or restored vintage cars. But my father gold-plated our cutlery. If *MTV Cribs* came to our house, my father would show off his knives, puffing and thumping his chest: "I bet Jay-Z and Beyoncé don't have these. Holler!"

He showed the knives off to my mother and lovingly put each knife back in the sleeve. A few days later, we sat around our kitchen table, slicing our steakies with our golden knives. Depending on how you look at it, we ate either like royalty or like pimps. A few months later I turned vegetarian.

Supposedly gold-plating wears off over time, but our knives are just as brilliant as ever, even after twenty years of broiled meats. My mother's jewelry still shines across a range of yellows and oranges. When I visit, I enjoy picking through her pieces. I particularly like untangling old bracelets and necklaces cast aside in shoe boxes and examining each one. You can't tell what's gold-plated and what's solid gold. Over the years, I've taken some of her old jewelry. It's like wearing a piece of my parents, which might sound sweet, but I take the gaudiest, most obnoxious things I can find. My last acquisition was a thick gold chain with a large white elephant that has gold tusks and a gold saddle with flashy blue, red, and green gems. I wore it to a bar and everyone tried it on and took photos, surprised it was my mother's and not from Canal Street, where you can find necklaces with giant dollar signs made of cubic zirconia. Later I found out that the necklace is real—the chain is solid gold. The elephant is made of ivory. Decades ago, my mother stopped wearing it because she thought it was gauche, and it is.

Eventually my father stopped gold-plating my mother's brooches and bangles. The gold was put to better use in the lab—be it for a job or just tossed in a drawer for retirement. Plus, tastes had changed. For the most part, my mother has stopped wearing gold. For my parents' fortieth wedding anniversary, my father got my mother a ring. It has a pearl and a few small diamonds, all set in a platinum band.

"Seriously, Dad. Bars of gold? That's nuts."

"Why nuts? It same as money."

"No it's not. If it were the same, we'd call it 'money' and not 'bars of gold.'"

"Annie." My father sat forward in his chair, the legs squeaking underneath him. "Promise that you and Mike take care of Mommy and split everything after I die."

I groaned. My father had had one brush with room-temperature roast beef and now he'd readied his estate and made arrangements for his death. The man was healthy; his cholesterol was good and his blood pressure was low, unlike those of his friends. He had many years ahead of him, no doubt filled with vacations and golf and moments of melodrama where he'd cough feebly and whisper that he was dying, when really all he needed was a snack and a nap. That's all anyone needs. There was plenty of time for existential crises; he still had time to ruminate over eternal oblivion and ponder how the individual self would enter a state of permanent unconsciousness. I knew he was planning ahead like a good father and husband (and scientist), but it was still a heavy trip—one I wasn't ready to take. I wished he'd gone to Olive Garden. "Yes, of course we'll split."

"Everything." He motioned around his lab, like a game show host presenting a prize: You've won your very own metallurgical laboratory! "Divide it all."

"Okay, but we don't actually want any of this."

"Then split what you not want."

"Fine, whatever. Just be sure to get rid of the chemicals before you die. We won't know how to deal with this stuff." I spied some jugs on the floor. They could have contained sulfuric acid or Mr. Clean, though only one of those got used in the lab.

"I just leave note." My father laughed.

I imagined a bottle labeled with a chemical formula and something about moles. There'd be a bright yellow DANGER: ACID label—the awesomely gruesome one that shows a test tube dripping on a hand with dissolving fingers. (In college, people stuck that on their dorm room walls and giggled while they came down from the other kind of acid.) Taped to the bottle would be long, highly detailed instructions on how to dispose of the contents. It would take me days to read it all and carry out the steps. Then it would dawn on me that there were hundreds of other bottles I'd have to address and discard properly. And, at some point, I'd accidentally make meth.

I looked around the lab, overwhelmed and annoyed that my father was preparing for his death, which in turn forced me to prepare too. "What about all these machines? What about that oven?"

The lab has an industrial furnace that's powerful enough to melt gold (of course), which has a melting point of about 1,947 degrees Fahrenheit. That's about 1,064 degrees Celsius or 1,337 degrees Kelvin, or about 851 degrees Réaumur, which is my favorite unit of temperature. It's used by some Italian cheese makers who make Parmesan. Opening the door to the furnace is like opening a door to the sun. I don't even understand what the oven's made out of. It seems like it should be made of fire, because that's the only thing that wouldn't melt.

"Just throw away."

"You can't just throw a furnace into a garbage can." I thought of tossing everything out—things that were useful and important to my father and then suddenly weren't because he was dead. How many trash cans would it take to hold a man's lifework?

"You figure it out. Everything be okay."

"Maybe for you, since you'll be gone." I laughed. Then stopped. Then laughed again. It's difficult for me to understand my dad's mortality; he's been alive for as long as I can remember. Death is not something I can accept. However, it is something I can ignore. "We don't have to talk about this now, Dad."

"Then when? Always think of future."

Eventually, my father melted his bars of gold and turned them into small pieces he could sell to manufacturers. He described the process over the phone, but I don't remember any of it. I was still reeling over the fact that I have a father who A) has bars of fucking gold and B) melts them. My friend's father is a pediatrician.

"Very beautiful, Annie. You should have seen—little gold nugget!"

I imagined a gleaming pile of gold, something you might find at the end of a rainbow. Only my father's treasure wasn't in a little black pot. It was in a drawer, along with a pair of rusty pliers, wayward shirt buttons, toenail clippers, and pencils with erasers that have hardened with age. My father finally got his nest egg ready to retire, but then decided to keep going. Mike joined him at the lab and now my father's training my brother to take the whole thing over, sometime in the future.

Hey, Neighbor!

Hi there! It's me again. It has been a few months now and I trust that you've settled into your apartment. Did you check out that new tapas bar that opened up on our street? The service is poor, the prices are high, and the food is repulsive. The good news is that they give you a lot of it. Have you seen Ad-Rock from the Beastie Boys yet? He lives around here. He has a cute dog—some kind of large, bearded hound. It has four legs and everything. I say that because there's a guy in our neighborhood who has a three-legged dog.

Anyway, I've noticed you still don't have curtains. This means you're not done moving in yet! Curtains can add a splash of color to every room. They can assert your style and personality—after all, shouldn't where you live be an extension of who you are? One of our neighbors has billowing lace (romantic!), one has plain blackout shades (utilitarian!), and another has neon orange (flashy!). One neighbor even has psychedelic kaleidoscope-print curtains (too flashy!). Mine happen to be white, and there's a big red stain on one of them. It's not blood, it's pomegranate juice, and it's a long story.

But curtains are much, much more than decoration. They are eyelids for your home. Can you imagine not having eyelids? You'd look constantly stunned. Eyelids are so important that some of our favorite animals have three of them, like dogs, cats, and aardvarks. Curtains allow your apartment to close its eyes and shut out the rest of the world. You need privacy when you come out of the shower or when you're clad in a towel and pawing through your closet. You need privacy when you put on an outfit and think, *No, no, this just won't do,* and then change into something else that's just as unsatisfying. You need time alone when you stand in front of the bathroom mirror in nothing but your bra and panties, brushing your hair, putting on makeup, plucking your eyebrows, squeezing a pimple, or addressing the mustache issue. These are just some of the things I do in the privacy of my own home.

And these are also some of the things I've seen you do.

Please don't be alarmed—I'm not spying on you! As you can see, our windows are rather close to each other. We could reach out and shake hands and actually meet one another, or we could set up Styrofoam-cup telephones, but that's going a little far. I'm not much of a phone person. I always close my curtains when I realize you need some "you time." We are both ladies here, so please don't feel threatened. I'm not being nosy; I'm just a neighbor trying to respect your space.

Now I'm going to share a story with you, and I hope you won't be horribly embarrassed. One sunny morning I opened my curtains, as I usually do, and I saw you, as I usually do. That particular morning, you were in bed. You were in bed with a gentleman friend. Both of you were naked. Eagles were spread. Soaring, really. Together, you were in what Shakespeare called a lovers' embrace, your limbs in compromising positions, though I do not think either of you was actually compromising anything. You both seem to be very athletic and in excellent reproductive health. I swear I was not peeping!

When I was in fourth grade, I saw Joey Marshall fall down a rocky ditch. I remember how his green Bermuda shorts were torn, and how his white socks and sneakers were soaked in blood. I remember how a gigantic flap of skin and tissue had been sheared away from his legs. His shins looked like strips of bacon. This image is burned into my memory and I think about him whenever I shave my legs. I guess what I'm saying is that there are things that cannot be unseen.

On several occasions, I've caught your gentleman friend naked, casually chatting on the phone. You're the only person I kind of know who has a landline. I'm not judging, merely making an observation—one made possible by the fact that you have no curtains. I've also caught him scratching his testicles while talking on the phone. Yes, this means your phone has traces of testicles on it. I am truly sorry to bear this news. To be clear, I'm not spying; my eyes just have bad timing. Also, you may want to clean the phone. It's been hot this past week, so I imagine the testicles in question are a bit on the swampy side.

Neighbor, this is all just a long-winded note to say that IKEA is having a sale. You can get two pairs of curtains for only $19! Everyone loves a good bargain, am I right?

Yours truly,
Annie

PS: Oh shit, George the super just told me you got mugged last month. So sorry about that. Glad you're safe.

MUGGING FOR THE CAMERA

One of my favorite photos shows me sitting in a high chair. I'm wearing a red party hat that makes me look like a garden gnome. My brother's next to me, also wearing a party hat, though his is red, white, and blue and matches his shirt perfectly—no doubt my mother's doing. She has a chapeau for every outfit and every occasion. She even has a set of visors that complement her golf wear (and they're all in the backseat of her car). Mike and I both have the same haircut, an overgrown bowl that frames our plump cheeks, and we're sitting at a table littered with paper plates and cups. It's unclear whose birthday it is, and naturally, no one in my family remembers. My brother, about four years old, is in deep concentration, his dark eyes zeroing in on the very important task of unwrapping an ice cream sandwich. His lips are parted and his tongue is sticking out ever so slightly. I'm staring at Mike, my eyes wide, my mouth open in a small *o*. I'm clearly fascinated by his intensity, and I just know he has something I don't, even though I have an ice cream sandwich right in front of me, in my own hands. I'm sure that two seconds after this photo was taken, I was calling for justice and demanding his dessert. You'd easily skip over this photo because it seems so clichéd—just another snapshot of kids with ice cream—but if you look closely, the details reveal a lot about Mike and me, and even my mother, who is the type of person who matches a paper party hat with an outfit. It's a funny but subtle moment that I don't see often in birthday photos of children, which are usually more slapstick and obvious—toddlers slathered in chocolate frosting, squealing kids with fistfuls of cake, etc.

Another photo shows me wearing bright, flowery overalls and a white top with poufy sleeves. I had a very tumultuous relationship with overalls as a child; I recall the sheer panic of trying to remove them so I could go to the bathroom and the stark humiliation of failing. Overall buckles require a degree in engineering to operate and I'm not sure why they're used in young children's clothing when Velcro is readily available. In the photo, I'm gazing moodily off into the distance, contemplating all that's happened in my three years of life, questioning everything: *How come Chap-Stick smells so good but tastes so bad? If chicken comes from chickens, why doesn't beef come from beefs? What, exactly, is a pooh?* My cheeks are full, my pigtails uneven. The photo is expertly composed—two lichen-speckled tree trunks frame the shot and you can see birch trees and a picnic table in the background in soft focus. The exposure is well balanced; there are no blinding light spots or muddy dark areas. You can see the wrinkles in my white shirt, as well as the details in my brown hair. It's a great photograph, one that could've come from the pages of a catalog—albeit one that sells overalls ready to be soaked in urine.

My father took both of these photos, but I wouldn't call him a talented photographer. I wouldn't even call him a photographer. He's more like a guy who takes pictures when the occasion calls for it. Still, he does have his moments. He used an old manual Canon, which he had bought before I was born. I remember posing and smiling stiffly and waiting as my father fussed with the lens, shutter, and aperture. He'd painstakingly tweak the dials to find a scientific combination of light and speed. By the time he took the photo, I'd be scowling impatiently. There are plenty of blurry snapshots of me where I've turned my head at the last minute or waved my arms in protest. Eventually, every time my father called for a picture, I'd scream like a little girl—because I was one—and run away. Then when I was in junior high, my father got a new camera (with autofocus). The old one remained untouched for years.

When I was home from college, I unearthed the Canon and marveled at its charm. There were dings and scratches on the body, and the black camera strap was soft and frayed from the years it had hung around my father's neck. The camera was complicated in the sense that it had more than one button. There were dials, rings, and knobs to push in, pull out, wind, and twist. Tiny little numbers were everywhere, in different colors, asking for attention. You couldn't just point and fire away. To use the Canon, you actually had to think and make decisions. It enabled you to be an artist and fail at it.

My father's camera had seen action around Korea and the States, with tours in Jeju-do, Seoraksan, Palm Springs, and Yellowstone. I decided to take it back with me to Berkeley and see if I had an eye for photography. I've always dreamed of having a hidden gift. Piano and math were areas I worked hard at and didn't come easily to me, so wouldn't it be nice to just pick up a camera and suddenly become Robert Frank? In the past, I'd tried archery to become William Tell. I'm sad to report that apples have nothing to fear.

"This is lens. You look through here to see picture."

"Oh God. Dad, I've used a camera before."

"This is focus. You turn to make picture clear. Not blurry."

"*I know,* you don't have to teach me."

"You push button to take picture."

"Enough. Stop."

"You push down."

"How else would you push a button? Thanks for the camera. I'm leaving to buy film."

"Wait, wait! I still have manual, let me find."

The next semester I enrolled in a photography class, along with dozens of coeds who were also exploring their Art. I quickly understood why it took my father so long to take a shot; the light meter worked sporadically and the shutter stuck. Plus, there was a small light leak in the body and the whole thing smelled like a sock drawer because that's where it came from. My pictures came out uneven; many were blurry and overexposed. Still, I used it anyway. Not just because of the nostalgia that came from shooting with my father's camera, but also because I couldn't afford a functional one. My photographs looked great if—and only if— you had cataracts.

I'm sitting on a bench along Bowditch Street, waiting for my friend to pick me up. It's an uncharacteristically sweltering afternoon, and I have positioned myself in a sliver of shade. It's the summer after I've graduated from college and I'm enjoying the freedom, though not the crippling anxiety, of growing up. I have my father's camera and my purse, a carpetbag with a pastel Southwestern pattern. My mother and I both prefer giant handbags, the kind that can fit books, gum, mints, two types of lotion, a sweater, a pair of shoes, a stack of napkins, Advil and Tylenol, and an entire drawer's worth of notepads and pens, including a detergent pen. There's also enough space for a bag of pretzels, a bottle of water, and a banana for when I get hungry. My friends tease me for carrying all this stuff, but when I fish out the Wet-Naps at picnics, don't think they don't take one.

I snap a few photos of nothing in particular and lean back on the bench and relax. The street is deserted even though I'm just a block from Telegraph Avenue, the main drag of Berkeley with thrift shops, record stores, and quaint boutiques that sell hand-blown glass bongs that look like dicks, all the way down to the nuts. There are apartment buildings and a large dorm around the corner, but everything is pleasantly quiet for a Sunday afternoon. It's one of those pockets of stillness that sometimes occur in a city. Off in the distance, I can hear a drum circle, the syncopated, cacophonous beats of hippies who spread their message of peace by disturbing it.

The hippies of Berkeley are a motley band of hominids who pretty much live up to the stereotypes. There are the bleeding-heart activists in vegan "leather" Birkenstocks who want to save things (children, Earth), stop things (drilling, death penalty), or free things (marijuana). There are also the more mystical hippies who explore "inner truths" and "align to the universal," and use hallucinogens and interpretive dance to find a version of God. Hate Man is a local antihero who encourages people to release their anger and live on the streets, in order to achieve peace or enlightenment or something along those lines. He wanders around itching his bushy beard, smoking cigarette butts off the sidewalk. Pink Man is a flamboyant unicyclist in a blinding pink unitard and matching cape.

He zips around the streets of Berkeley, performing tricks and singing a message of love and joy. He happens to have a history of child molestation. What this all means is that Berkeley is a loud place with a lot of energy—spiritual or otherwise—and one unicycle. The body stink of cumin lingers in the air, along with wafts of weed.

I sit and wait for my friend, savoring a moment of peace where no one is asking me to sign a petition or join a youth group that may or may not be a cult. I stretch and yawn. I think about my future. And then I stop thinking about my future because it's too stressful and it's not like I'm going to figure it out right now. What I can figure out is lunch and possibly dinner, though I shouldn't get too ambitious. I see two guys amble up the sidewalk. One has bleached spiky hair and an enormous plug stretching out each ear. They're the size of bathtub stoppers, and if he took them out, his ears would look like vaginas. But the guy's not quite a gutter punk; his attire lacks the suitable number of safety pins and patches for street cred. The real gutter punks of Berkeley wear jackets that are made of 2 percent leather and 98 percent metal studs, and the same could be said of their faces. Even if it's ninety degrees outside, they'll be dressed in full leather, sitting on a sunny patch of gutter and asking for change to buy beer. But this fellow on the street is less punk and more guy-who's-trying-too-hard-but-not-hard-enough. His ripped white shirt seems recently laundered, which isn't very punk. He's Punk Lite.

His friend is short and skinny and wears a faded baseball cap low over his eyes. He has on the ubiquitous black T-shirt—it's the thing anyone can wear if they don't want to be naked—and his dark blue shorts are hung well below his hips. With every step his shorts slip lower and lower, and with every step the battle against gravity becomes more and more indecent. I'm not even sure if they're technically shorts. Since they hang down to mid-calf, they're more like capris or clam diggers. So while he's trying hard to look tough, he is essentially wearing the same thing ladies wear to yoga class.

Punk Lite walks up to a pay phone behind me. Saggy Bottoms approaches my bench.

He snatches my bag and my camera. He runs.

I freeze, trying to grasp what just happened: I had stuff, and now I don't. In the Road Runner cartoons, there's a moment when Wile E. Coyote catches a live bomb in his hand. He looks at it and then stares into the camera with a gut-wrenching look of defeat. He holds up a sign that says HELP!, a sad and hopeless plea to the kids at home who are no doubt rooting for the stupid bird that looks nothing like the roadrunners I saw growing up. After a beat, the bomb explodes, and Wile E. Coyote gets barbecued, dark smoke rising from his charred fur. Then the Road Runner—that prick—slips past with a "Beep! Beep!" which is the cartoon equivalent of the middle finger.

I sense Punk Lite looming nearby. I don't know what he plans on doing with me, but it probably won't involve mani-pedis. I jump from my bench and I run. In the direction of the thief. I see him, his cap bobbing up and down as he's racing up the street.

"YOU FUCKING ASSHOLE!"

I yell and holler and scream as I chase him. No one is around. Berkeley is a city of over a hundred thousand people, and there are over thirty-five thousand students enrolled at the university. And not a single one of them is on the street. There isn't even a car. It's as if we're the last two people left on Earth, and it just so happens that one of us is an asshole. To be clear, that person is not me.

"GIVE ME BACK MY BAG!"

I don't know if Punk Lite is behind me, but I don't hear any footsteps other than mine. I fixate on the target ahead of me. In my mind, I catch up to him and tackle him. We crash into a fruit stand, blueberries thrown in the air like confetti. I pin his arms behind his back and I use my belt to restrain him. Then I read him his rights and kick him while he's down because I am both the good and bad cop.

"STOP! STOP! YOU FUCKING FUCK!"

I continue to run. My heart is exploding, each thud matching up with my shoes hitting the pavement. My hands are in tight fists; I can feel my nails dig into my palms. My arms swing and pump at my sides as I'm sprinting up the empty street. He's a block and a half ahead of me, but I'm closing in on him. I am in the best shape of my life; I run four times a week. More importantly, my bag is unwieldy and weighing the thief down and his shorts are sagging so much that he has to slow down to hike them back up.

"COME BACK HERE! GIVE IT BACK!" Never once in the long, decorated history of robbery has the victim cried, "Give it back!" and the perp replied, "Oh sure, here you go." But I say it anyway.

He's now a block ahead of me, but if he turns a corner, I might lose him. He approaches an intersection, where, finally, there's another human. There's a guy on the corner, about to cross the street.

"STOP HIM! STOP HIM! HE STOLE MY BAG!"

The guy quickly looks at me and the perp holding my purse. It's clearly a bag only a girl would carry; it might as well be made of tampons. The guy lunges for the mugger and catches his shirt. The thief drops everything, shakes him off, and runs again.

I reach the intersection, slowing down just enough to scoop

up my stuff, and continue the chase. I see the thief heading toward a row of storefronts, where people are shopping and strolling at a leisurely pace. I make my plan to tackle him and crash through the window of a barbershop, which will be empty because in Berkeley, men wear their hair in buns.

Suddenly, I feel a hand grab my arm and pull me backward. I yell and jerk my arm away. "NO! GET THE FUCK AWAY FROM ME!"

"Stop! Stop!"

I feel another hand on my shoulder hold me back. I fight it off. "LET ME GO!"

"HEY! What do you think you're doing?"

I get spun around. It's the guy who grabbed the thief.

"What are you thinking? Stop!" He doesn't let go of my arm until I quit struggling, which I do.

I'm wheezing. Everything is pounding, my heart, lungs, ears. My eyeballs throb with flashes of white and red. My fingers are still closed in tight fists and my toes are curled and gripping the insides of my shoes. I'm shaking. It is the fight-or-flight response and I want to do both.

"Are you okay?"

"*No.* That guy . . . is getting . . . away . . ." I'm dizzy, so I hunch over and focus on something to steady myself. He's wearing Tevas.

"Shhh, shhh." He pats my back gently. "Calm down. Breathe."

"I'm . . . breathing." I gasp and sputter. "I need . . . to get him . . ."

"No you don't."

"Yes . . . I do." I look up in the direction my mugger escaped, wondering if I can catch up even though he's out of sight. My chest heaves; my entire body is greedy for air.

"Hey now, you got your stuff back. Be cool." He stares at me incredulously. He's about my age, wearing a faded tie-dye shirt and a thick hemp necklace with shells. "You don't know what he might do."

I start to protest but cough instead. My throat is dry from the jets of heated air blasting from my lungs.

"Relax, calm down. You're okay."

"I know." I keep panting.

"Focus." He raises his arms to waist level and touches the tips of his index finger and thumb on each hand. "Breathe in . . . breathe out . . ." He closes his eyes and inhales and exhales deeply. He is in a deep meditative trance, tapping into his chakras. If he started chanting or om-ing, I wouldn't be surprised, only embarrassed. "In . . . out . . ."

I stare at him in disbelief. I do not wish to meditate. Nor do I wish to find the "inner presence of an awakened living" or go on any "transcendent journey of the heart" described on the flyers posted around campus. What I want to do is hunt down this malicious piece of shit like a vigilante who Does Not Give a Fuck. I'll wallop him in the nose because that's how you stun sharks into submission, and while he's writhing around on the floor in a modern dance routine, I'll deliver a sermon about the law and human decency and the importance of a belt. Then I'll grab a fork and stick it in his leg. The wound won't be fatal, but every single time he sees a fork, he'll remember how he messed with me. Also, people will ask, "Yo, what happened to your leg?" and he'll have to explain and everyone will laugh at him and be impressed with the fact that I actually carry a fork in my purse. Namasté, bitch.

Of course, the reality is that the perp could kill me, either by gun or by knife to the eye. But then my heart will be donated to a little girl who'll vow to avenge my death. She'll master five forms of martial arts and perfect a hybrid Krav Maga/Muaythai maneuver that'll be named in her honor. In the final showdown, she'll bust out "the Kaitlyn" and deliver swift justice. Peace will be restored. Doves will be released.

"Do you feel better?"

I finally begin to catch my breath, though my legs feel gelatinous. "No. I mean, yes."

"You're okay."

"I know. Thanks for helping, and thanks for keeping me from doing something stupid." My words are inadequate, unable to communicate the sense of appreciation I feel. It's like when someone bakes brownies for a team of firefighters who have saved an entire neighborhood from an inferno: Hope you like dark-chocolate fudge—are walnuts okay? It's possible that this guy saved my life, though I'd like to think that the thief's life was actually saved. "Thanks, really." I feel even more heat rise to my face.

"It's the least I can do, friend. Do you want to call the police?"

I start to say yes, but I stop myself. What could the police do? Listen to my description and find this asshole in a sea of guys who look just like him? Yes, officer, he had on a cap and shorts and shoes—I hope you find him! The police have better things to do, like go after thieves who actually stole stuff—and got away with said stuff. According to the crime bulletins, the rate of auto theft in Berkeley is over 100 percent worse than the rate for the entire state of California. I know my case is hopeless, but at least it has a happy ending as far as misdemeanors go. So maybe it should just go unreported and fade into the dark figure of crime. Plus, I'm embarrassed. I know better. I have friends who've gotten laptops stolen or their places burglarized. The thought of losing my camera—as borderline nonfunctional as it is—makes me heartbroken, which makes me feel even more ashamed that I didn't secure it better. I feel like a chump. The chance of becoming a victim of property crime in Berkeley is one in sixteen (in New York City, it's one in fifty).

I shrug. "What's the point? He's gone."

"I hear you." The Good Samaritan nods and smiles. "S'all good. The universe will take care of the rest." He says good-bye and turns to leave, not before flashing the peace sign.

"What? Oh my God." My mother sputters into the phone. "You *chase?"*

"I know, I know . . ."

"He have gun? Knife?"

"No, nothing like that, I don't think."

"So he just walk up and take? Like *nabbeun nom* on playground?" *Nabbeun nom* literally translates to "bad guy," but it refers to a bastard, a dirtbag, a sleazeball, a low-life cockloaf, etc.

"But I got it all back." I'm sheepish, which is a funny word because sheep aren't sheepish. They're dumb.

"Annie . . ."

My mother is silent. I can hear the sizzle of something frying. She is thinking. She is preparing a lecture or, more accurately, a tirade about safety and impulse and how a stupid split-second decision can affect the rest of my life. There'll be touches of dramatic flair: "If you die, what Mommy and Daddy do?" She has a narrative all worked out:

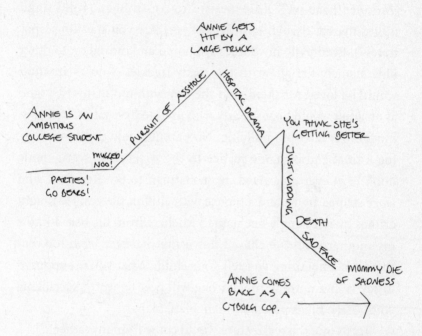

I can hear the scrape of a drawer opening and the rattling of silverware.

"I know it was dumb to run after him. You don't have to tell me."

"Anne, you be careful." She's quiet again.

"That's it? That's all you have to say?"

"What I can say? You already know. *Ayoo, nabbeun nom.* His mommy must be so disappoint." My mother laughs. "Maybe you teach him lesson."

There's just a hint of pride in my mother's voice. In elementary school, kids would push me, hide my books, and call me Chinese, as if being Chinese were a bad thing. I'm sure whenever they enjoyed the orange chicken from Empire Szechuan they thought of me and how I was such a loser. My mother yelled at me to keep it together: "*Ddook!* No cry! You tell them, '*Nuh nen babo ya!*'" This means "You're an idiot." I did stand up for myself, though to little success ("Are you speaking Japanese?"). Eventually my bullies got bored and moved on to other kids, namely the girl with too many freckles, who as an adult would be loved for them, and the boy with too many zits, who as an adult would be just a guy who used to have zits. Obviously, mugging is far from bullying. No parent would condone chasing a thief and bringing justice to the streets like every comic book hero ever conceived, from Batman to the Red Bee, who wore striped tights and a blouse with chiffon sleeves. He fought crimes by releasing a bee named Michael from his belt. I know my mother would've chased down that *nabbeun nom* too, but that's not something you tell your child. What you're supposed to say is that nothing in your bag will ever be worth sacrificing your safety, life is precious, blah, blah, blah.

Turns out, the real lecture would come from my father.

"Why you chase, Annie? Very stupid. Very, very stupid."

"I know, I know, you don't have to tell me."

"You had lot of money with you?"

"Yeah." I have a part-time job at the university housing office. It pays $5.15 an hour, which means $5.15 is a lot of money. "Eight dollars."

"That's it? That all you have?" My father gasps.

"I have money in the bank. It's not like I carry it all with me." Though, I could very easily, in my change purse.

"How you can survive with only eight dollar?"

"By not spending more than eight dollars."

"Annie, always carry cash."

"I do, and I also have a bank that carries cash for me."

"Always have twenty dollar in you wallet, just in case."

"So the guy could've made off with twenty dollars instead of eight?"

"Annie, think. What if there's emergency?"

"You mean, like, if someone mugged me?" I sniff. "Then I wouldn't have *any* money."

"What if you stuck somewhere?"

"Like where? In some magical place that doesn't have any ATMs?"

"Eight dollar won't help you."

"Neither will twenty."

"You need better job. What you going to do? You graduate college. Now what you do for career?"

"Dad, did you miss the part where I got mugged? I had your camera."

"That camera is junk. No one care about that."

I start to protest but I stop. I know he's right, but I still see the camera of my childhood. My father sees nothing but my future.

A week later, I go to the darkroom and develop the roll that was in my camera when I was unsuccessfully mugged. It's black-and-white film, which I rarely use because it's expensive—one roll costs about the same as my hourly wage. This means that each snapshot is equal to a folder I had to file or a phone call I had to answer. I always agonize over pressing the shutter button. Is this picture really worth listening to someone complain about her housing assignment? Do I really want to take a photo of these flowers, and isn't it pointless in black and white? Wait, I don't even like flowers. It usually takes me a long time to finish a roll of black-and-white film—so long that I forget what I shot. Looking through my negatives is like coming in and out of amnesia—oh yes, I remember this guy on the street with the parrot, but I don't remember this party; where am I and what's up with the dude in the pig mask?

This time, however, I burned through the film as fast as I could. I wanted to see my negatives and relive that Sunday afternoon. Maybe I caught the *nabbeun nom* and his accessory on film as they walked up the street. Maybe the camera went off in Saggy Bottoms's face when he grabbed it. Then I can plaster his face all over town: HAVE YOU SEEN THIS UNPLEASANT TURD? I turn on the light box and look.

I find a shot of my friend. She's sitting outside on the steps of a building. She has a squirt gun, which she's holding up to her eye and carefully aiming even though it's totally unnecessary. All she has to do is point the gun in a general direction, spray the area down, and watch people squeal and squirm because water is so dangerous that you can only come in contact with it when you're naked or close to it. My friend's dark hair is slightly windswept, giving her a Pantene vibe, but it's ruined by a supernova of white glare on her forehead. It looks like she's wearing a headlamp, ready to go spelunking. I clearly didn't meter properly, and, as a result, ruined her face.

The next picture shows garbage on the sidewalk. There's a crushed paper cup, wads of napkins, and a paper bag. There's also a piece of food that is either a partially eaten donut or a partially digested hot dog, both of which I don't particularly care for in their uneaten states. I don't know why I took this shot; maybe I found beauty in it, somewhere. I certainly don't see the beauty now. I see a pile of fetid trash feeding insects that have more legs than necessary, plus wings. If there's one thing insect anatomy tells us, it's that they're good at getting around. The picture's contrast is too flat and the texture is lost, which makes the garbage look mushier and even less appetizing. I'm sure that in the future, I will look back fondly at this and say, "Oh, I remember this mound of rubbish—that was incredible."

I move on to the next frame, which shows the windows of a drab apartment building, an organized grid of rectangles. They're opened to varying heights, and the windows look like winking or squinting eyes. It's a fine photograph except for the fact that it's boring. I recognize the apartment building; it's a few blocks from Bowditch Street. I eagerly look at the next shot. It's a large eucalyptus tree that was directly across from where I was sitting. When I was little, I thought koalas lived in the eucalyptus trees in our neighborhood. Then when I was older, I learned this was not the case. Then when I was older still, I learned that koalas are actually feisty creatures that do not want to be cuddled or spooned. I take a closer look. It's just a tree on a corner. There's no sign of a *nabbeun nom*, not even a shadow. Still, the picture is satisfactory. It's hard to take a bad shot of a tree; they never blink or grimace. The leaves were rustling as I took the shot, so some of them are blurry. Part of the tree looks smeared, as if it's being erased.

The frame after that shows an accordion player on a cobblestone street in San Francisco. His jeans are ripped at the knees and he's wearing giant glasses that take up most of his face. The bellows of the accordion are white and contrast nicely with the dark buttons and keys. Low houses frame each side of the picture and the curving pattern of the cobblestones gives a sense of motion and texture. The musician is enjoying his life, serenading and annoying whoever will listen. I recall his being not a very good player but a rather enthusiastic one. He had played a tune that sounded exactly like a car horn being tortured by an angry, drunk harmonica.

I laugh by myself in the darkroom. Somewhere between the

eucalyptus tree and the accordion player, there's an entire story that's completely missing. My photos just jump from one moment to the next, with no hint of what happened in between. There are no ellipses between the frames to show that something's been omitted. A lifetime could've passed between the two moments. I could've discovered a species of armored catfish in Suriname or taken up fencing or even celebrated my fiftieth birthday. At the very least, I could've mastered "the Kaitlyn." I print the photo of the accordion player because it's the only one worth printing from my roll.

The one thing that the *nabbeun nom* did manage to steal is my sense of security. I walk around the city suspicious and anxious, on the lookout for roving bands of thugs. I am ready for action and I'll fight if I have to—hopefully they'll attack one by one like in the kung-fu movies. Everywhere I go, I search for Saggy Bottoms and Punk Lite on the street and in the gutters. I look for their faces in record stores, in bars, and even in line at Krishna Copy Center. Because sometimes people with loose pants need to send a fax. If and when I find them, I'll tail them home (because they live together obviously), and in the middle of the night, I'll find an open window and release a mischief of rats. They won't carry the bubonic plague, but they'll spread some other disease that involves unpredictable, explosive diarrhea through the mouth. Then I'll call the police.

I start wearing my purse with the strap across my body, clutching its contents close to my stomach like a football—a massive football that holds moisturizers and magazines. Even when I sit down at a restaurant, I keep the strap secured across my chest, like a seat belt, with the bag dangling next to my seat. It looks uncomfortable because it is. A friend teaches me how to loop a purse strap around the leg of a chair or table to keep it secure. It's a tip she learned in Brazil, where purse-snatching is the third most popular activity after soccer and being good-looking. I steer clear of Bowditch Street, which is problematic because the housing office is there, and that's where I work. I go out of my way to use the back entrance just so I can avoid the bench where Saggy Bottoms nabbed my stuff. The bench reminds me of my stupidity and I can hear it taunt me; I am being bullied by a piece of furniture. My mother would be "so disappoint" if she knew.

Over time, the scumbags fade away between two frames of film. I use Bowditch Street again and even enjoy it. During breaks at work, I sit on the bench and eat the snacks in my purse. I relax, though not too much. Even today, whenever I'm sitting somewhere, I'll periodically glance at my stuff to make sure it's still there, and for the past fifteen years, it always has been. Sometimes I imagine a thief snatching my bag and running through the streets of New York, weaving through cabs, buses, and people walking their puggles on rhinestone leashes. I chase after the *nabbeun nom,* shoving strollers out of my way and hurdling over traffic barricades like the decorated Olympian I am. But then I wonder if I'd really chase a mugger down now—I'm fully aware that all the crap in my bag is just that: crap. And I think, *Yes, yes I would.* I can't really see myself standing on Broadway, dumbfounded, as some jackass runs off with a half-filled coffee punch card and two tubes of lipstick.

After I got my first job out of college, I bought myself a new manual camera, and after I got a promotion, I made the switch to digital. The last photo I took shows a mourning dove. I used a Canon, but a digital one. The bird is fat and brown with dark speckles on its wings. It's a cheeky bastard that wakes me up every dawn with its plaintive calls for a spouse. It's perched on my fire escape, and behind it you can see my neighbor's windows, which now have curtains, finally. I could print this picture out and put it next to the one of the accordion player—there'd be quite the ellipses between them. But I lost that photo long ago, when I moved to New York. As for my father's Canon, I still have it, and it's still broken.

Dear Caesars Palace,

Aut Caesar aut nihil! Either Caesar or nothing!

The Roman Empire is among my top three favorite empires, not that it's a competition. It's right up there with the Ottoman Empire and the Inland Empire, which is an area of Southern California. It's where you can find Rancho Cucamonga, which is what I'd name my dog if I ever got one. The Roman Empire was a riveting period of history and I approve of any civilization that has gladiators, aqueducts, and a horny god who got a lady pregnant by raining on her. Also, togas.

Caesars Palace, I'm impressed by your dedication to the Roman Empire theme. No detail is overlooked, from the busts of vestal virgins to the bacchanal buffets. The architecture is successfully ancient Roman in flavor, which is to say there are a lot of columns. The ceilings are high and vaulted, decorated with gilded grapes, laurels, and mythological beasts. Nothing says ancient Rome like a guy with a horse's ass. I do like the replica of *Nike of Samothrace,* though it seems a bit cruel to put the goddess of victory anywhere near a slot machine. I also enjoy the many frescoes of cherubs floating above bucolic Roman settings. Whenever I see a painting, I like to imagine what's beyond the scene, out of view. What might be there? Maybe it's a group of dancing nymphs or humble merchants peddling urns. Maybe it's a gigantic arena where two armies—each of two thousand gladiators, two hundred horses, and twenty elephants—are fighting to the bloody death, in the name of entertainment. This was actually something that happened in Rome. Now, two thousand years later, a gladiator opens the door for you in the middle of the Mojave Desert. It's a gentle reminder of how far Rome has fallen.

As I walk through your hotel, I can just imagine Brutus stabbing Julius Caesar and then running over to the Colosseum to catch Céline Dion in concert. I can see Marc Antony lounging poolside in a cabana, ordering a refreshing wine spritzer. I can picture Vespasian strolling through the Forum Shops, perhaps buying gladiator sandals at Balenciaga. Then, before heading to the Cheesecake Factory, he stops to watch the Festival Fountain shows. He gets confused. He gets angry. Also bored. So, he orders executions because that's what emperors do when they're bored. These talking-gods shows are tragedies. They are missteps in an otherwise magical experience. They're an affront to not just the Roman Empire, but to all empires, including the largely unsung Akkadian. There's no reason to have not one, but two different monstrosities that involve fountains and animatronic statues.

One show starts with Bacchus announcing something—I don't know what, he's incoherent. He seems drunk, which is fitting, but I don't think that's the intention. Or is it? Apollo plays the lyre and Venus makes it rain, I think. Pluto's there too, but ever since he stopped being a planet, I stopped caring about him. The other show features King Atlas's entitled children, who brag about their powers. One claims she can control the tides; obviously, she's never heard of the moon. At some point there's an argument and the resolution is to sink Atlantis, which is actually how I solve my problems too. Water erupts from the ancient Roman fountains, accompanied by ancient Roman flashing neon lights. Flames burst from the statues, but it's not very dramatic—it's in a mall after all. I get the feeling these shows are meant for the whole family to enjoy, particularly children under the age of ten. But you should understand these animatronic gods do not interest kids. You'd know just by hearing their chilling screams when the statue wearing a loincloth waves a torch and warns of destruction. The kids who aren't crying are playing with their iPads.

My dear Caesars Palace, everyone knows that Las Vegas isn't for children. So why try to appeal to them—and fail? Why even bother? Sin City is for debauched bachelor and bachelorette parties, and for people who enjoy losing money and drinking, and getting lap dances while losing money and drinking. It's for appletinis, kiwitinis, espressotinis, and other drinks that might as well be served in a toilet because that's where most of it ends up. Vegas is for bad behavior, bad choices, and even worse hangovers, which is why there's a high concentration of people who woo-hoo out of limo windows. There are bars and clubs called Krave, Tabú, and Joystixx—proof that the city is too drunk to spell. Vegas is for prostitution and illegal drugs and places where you can shoot an AK-47 and a grenade launcher, as in a gun that actually launches grenades. That explode.

You know what else isn't for children? The Roman Empire. It was a time when emperors ordered innocents to be eaten by lions because no criminals were left to be eaten. Nero ordered his own mother to be executed and then exiled his wife because she couldn't bear him a child, and also because he was a jerk. Domitian took his niece as a mistress, who then died during an abortion. Caligula ran a brothel out of the palace and ordered executions by sawing. People were hung upside down and then sawed in half, lengthwise, starting from the groin. It just was a horrible, horrible time. But hey, casinos are fun!

I see no reason for you to appeal to kids. They have plenty of other places to go—for example, anywhere else that's not a bar. So forget them. Embrace the Palace as a grown-up's playground for drunken revelries. Then make animatronic shows that actually draw crowds and keep them interested. Some suggestions:

- Re-create the time when Jupiter had a really bad headache and so Vulcan cleaved open his skull and then— whoa—Minerva came out.

- Show Hercules putting on the poisoned Shirt of Nessus and then throwing himself into a pyre. It's a part of his story that everyone always forgets, but there's a happy ending: He becomes Arnold Schwarzenegger.

- Depict Ixion being punished on a spinning wheel of fire that never stops. This would involve a laser show.

Obviously my suggestions make for excellent adult entertainment in the spirit of ancient Rome, only without the beheadings. I'm sure you find these ideas refreshing and educational, and I'm pleased to say that I have more. Please contact me to discuss this further.

Ab imo pectore,
(From the bottom of my heart,)
Annie Choi

DING DONG DITCHED

"Hey, Mom. I'm here!"

"Anne! Where you are?"

"Baggage claim B."

"Really?"

"You sound surprised. Where are you?"

"I be late . . . I thought you come in at three thirty."

"No, my flight came in at two forty-five." I looked at my watch. It was three o'clock.

"Oh."

"So where are you? On the freeway?" My parents live about forty-five minutes away from the airport, without traffic. I paused. "Wait, is that the bathtub I hear?"

"No . . ."

"Mom, are you taking a bath?"

"No, no, why I do that?"

I heard the faint but unmistakable squeak of a faucet. "Holy shit, you're taking a bath! Did you forget I was coming?"

"No, I not forget."

"Seriously?" I dropped my bag on the airport floor. "Mom, it's *Christmas!*"

"Merry Christmas!"

"I reminded you I was coming last night. I gave you my flight info again."

"I didn't check message. But I not forget. Mike pick you up. He must be late."

"But you just said *you* were running late."

"No, I didn't."

"Yes, you did."

"Mike be there."

"Oh really?" I hung up and immediately dialed my brother. "Hey, where are you?"

"At home."

"I fucking knew it! I'm at the airport. Mom said you were going to pick me up."

"Really? No one told me."

"Total bullshit." I sat down on a chair. This was going to take a while. Some kids next to me were playing with their Christmas toys and roughhousing dangerously close to me. I stared them down. Kids take work. You have to feed them and get them out of trouble, and at some point, you have to pick them up at an airport. Or not. "I'm going to kill someone."

"Kill Mom, this isn't my fault."

"Look, is anyone going to pick me up? I'm at the airport, waiting around like some kind of asshole." The kids stared at me. I lowered my voice. "I'm causing a scene."

"Okay, okay, I'll leave now."

"Wait! I'm at Burbank."

"Good to know, I was going to drive to LAX."

"Goddamn it!"

"Relax, Annie, relax."

I hate it when people tell me to relax or calm down. It makes me feel like my batshit outbursts aren't warranted. The last thing I want to do is take a chill pill or take it easy or keep it mellow, man. Especially when I'm at the airport, on Christmas, watching other people get picked up by their loved ones, hugging and kissing and wiping away tears. I, too, had tears—while waiting for Mike, an easy-listening rendition of "Silent Night" played over the airport speakers. It was one of the easiest and hardest things I've ever had to hear.

I burst through the door. My mother was there waiting.

"Anne, I thought you coming tomorrow."

"No, I came today. See? I'm here." I scoffed. "You totally forgot about me. On Christmas."

"I not forget."

My mother directed me to her "Landmarks of Korea" wall calendar, an oversized poster featuring shrines, palaces, and Seoul Tower, which looks like a wedding cake stuck on a jousting lance. She pointed to the spot for December 26, 2009. In a haphazard scrawl with a mix of Korean and English, it said ANNIE, BURBANK, 3:30. "*Ayoo*, see, Anne? I not forget. I write down you come tomorrow."

"Give her credit. She got your name and the airport right." Mike laughed. "She got half."

"You got fifty percent. You get an F." I rolled my eyes. "I *always* come on Christmas. Like, for the past ten years."

"Annie's right." Mike nodded matter-of-factly. "It's the only holiday tradition we have."

"Right, right." She frowned. "I driving when you tell me and I write down when I get home."

"Did you get home two days later or something?"

Mike laughed. My mother glared at him.

"I'm allowed to laugh. Calm down."

She pointed to the kitchen table filled with food. "I make *doenjang jjiggae*. You here now, so eat." She pulled out a chair for me. "I'm sorry, I make mistake. I never forget my only daughter!"

"You're kidding, right?"

Christmas is not a big deal in our family, which is surprising given my mother's love of all things Jesus. You'd think that someone who collects Jesus clocks and Jesus teaspoons and Jesus paperweights would celebrate his birthday with much gusto. When my parents were growing up in Seoul, Christmas was just a thing that happened, a label on a calendar. It was a holiday, sure, but a low-carb, fat-free holiday, one without much fanfare. It was common for couples to spend Christmas together, the way they spend Valentine's Day here in the States. Korea is traditionally Buddhist, and if you walk the streets of Seoul, you'll see temples sandwiched between malls and luxury hotels. But now every December, Seoul explodes with decorated trees and twinkling lights and voracious consumerism, just like the Western world does. In every department store there's cancerous holiday music and a *Santa harabojee,* which translates to "Santa grandfather." He looks like Santa as we know him, except sometimes he wears blue and white, which is confusing since those are the Hanukkah colors. I'm pretty sure Santa's not Jewish—I doubt he hosts a Passover seder and hides the *afikoman.* But that's a minor detail. Every holiday season, *Santa harabojee* brings gifts and yuletide cheer and lies to children. However, my parents didn't grow up with all this fuss, so for them—and by extension me and my brother—Christmas is just another day. A day with its own soundtrack, but otherwise unexceptional.

There actually was a time when Christmas was something special in our family, something to wet my pants over (and then hide it from my mother). I can remember four or five years when we got a tree. It was the same tree each time. It was plastic but looked and smelled like real pine, the same way a car freshener smells like real pine. The "trunk" of the tree was a PVC pipe spray-painted green. It had holes that spiraled upward and each was labeled with a letter and number, B19, F23, P2. When it was time to assemble the tree, my father would call out the letter and number, and Mike and I would rummage through the boxes to find the plastic branch with the matching label. It was like a game of bingo. I'm not sure why my father chose a fake tree over a real one; he's a man who appreciates plants. But I was six and didn't care. You could've put a sprig of parsley in front of me and I would've enjoyed decorating it. Our family put a mountain of gifts under the tree, displayed our holiday cards, and hung a fake wreath with fake fruit on our front door—the one no one used because everyone entered the house through the garage, even guests. On the bookshelf, we put up wooden blocks that spelled "noel" (or "leon" if you put them together wrong like I did). We adorned the piano with pieces of plastic holly and a Santa puppet I made out of a paper bag, something my mother didn't care for because the glitter and sequins would come off and make a mess. My puppet looked less like Santa and more like a drag queen. My favorite decoration was a set of snow-covered cottages, each a different color. I was very interested in cottages since exciting things seemed to happen there, like wolves eating girls and bears eating porridge. My brother and I had stockings on our nightstands, and they'd be full of treats when we woke up on Christmas morning. These treats looked suspiciously similar to Halloween candy— Smarties and fun-sized Snickers. My mother rationed out our Halloween candy in a very miserly fashion, so it was possible she still had some left at the end of December. But when you're little, candy is candy, even if it tastes like plaster. We strung lights in the windows that stayed up until February, and I played "Here Comes Santa Claus" on the piano poorly. We ate a canned ham. It was all very Norman Rockwell, except for the miniature stone pagoda in the foyer. My father stuck flashing lights inside of it, so it was like a Buddhist disco.

Then when I was in fourth grade, my parents decided to stop with the tree and the decorations.

"It just too much work, Annie." My mother looked apologetic. But not too apologetic.

"No it's not, we all help."

"So messy. Everything is everywhere in house. I get such a headache."

My father nodded. "You don't want Mommy to get headache, do you?"

"But it's Christmas," I whined. "We're *supposed to* have a tree."

"Anne, Christmas *supposed to* be about family." My mother tsk-tsked me. Though whenever she tsks, she only does it once. Tsk.

"Our family wants a tree." I pouted and looked to Mike. "This is so unfair."

He shrugged. "It doesn't matter." Mike was now in junior high, knee-deep in science fiction and Dungeons & Dragons and his encyclopedias. "What's the point? It's just another day."

"What about lights? Can we at least put up lights?"

"Lights in garage. I don't know where." My father shook his head firmly. "We don't need."

"What about gifts?"

"Okay, we can do gift. But only one," my father said, acquiescing.

"Only one," my mother echoed, "Exactly this many." She held up one finger.

And so at the tender age of ten, I learned the true meaning of Christmas, which is to say, disappointment. Eventually I got used to it and learned to explain our lack of holiday spirit in three words or less ("Too much work" or "We stopped"). Still, I couldn't help feeling a little left out. My friends and their families celebrated Christmas competitively, but in a contest where everyone's a winner, like the third-grade science fair. Everywhere I looked it was Christmas—at school, in stores, around streetlamps. My dentist's office was decorated with a menorah and a nativity scene, a reminder that both Jews and Christians battle gingivitis. Every house in our neighborhood twinkled. And yet our house remained dark.

When I was in seventh grade, our family moved and we threw out all of the holiday decorations, which had mildewed in their boxes. By then I wasn't interested in Christmas. I was brooding over my destiny, a floppy-haired boy named Jason who carried a skateboard but never rode it. My brother, now a sophomore, cared even less. He was getting teased in school for his love of anime, comics, and historical artillery. Christmas in our family was dead, or at least left behind in a manger.

Then a year later, my parents found the holiday spirit elsewhere—at church. My mother was getting increasingly active, taking on leadership roles, sitting on committees, organizing events, going to parties, gossiping. She got very good at spotting plastic surgery. My father tagged along to events because that's what husbands are supposed to do and, as my mother pointed out, it looks "bad to God" if only one of them shows up to mass. Mike and I had long since bowed out of church.

One Christmas morning my mother woke me up in a panic.

"Anne! Anne!" She shook my shoulder vigorously. There are things that are supposed to be shaken (a drink, your money-maker) and things that are not (bombs, children).

"What? What! Are you okay?"

"Help Mommy! Get up." She yanked the covers off of me. "I need dance song."

"What?" I yanked them back over me. "What are you talking about?" I glared at her with one eye. The other was stuck closed with sleep.

"Dance song, you know famous dance song." She hummed a few bars. It could've been anything, "Twinkle, Twinkle Little Star" or the national anthem of Bulgaria.

"I don't know it. I'm too tired for this." I put the pillow over my head.

"Anne. Help."

"Okay, fine. What are the words?"

"I don't know, it not in English."

"*Ohhh,* that song."

"You know?" She threw the pillow off my head.

"No, I'm being sarcastic. There are a lot of songs not in English. I don't know them because they're not in English. Give me my pillow back."

"It famous song, with dance." She stretched each arm outward and then crossed them over her chest. She wagged her backside.

I stared, appalled. "Oh my God, the Macarena?"

"Yes! Macaroon! I need music. You have to buy now!"

My clock read seven thirty. That's A.M., as in *ante meridiem,* Latin for "before midday and not the right time to discuss the dance sensation of 1996." It was 2001.

"It's Christmas. I want to sleep like the baby Jesus."

"Anne!" She threw the covers off of me again. "You have to find for Mommy or else I get trouble! I teach everyone at party tonight."

"Everyone already knows it."

"Not old people."

"Haven't old people been through enough?"

"Dance is fun, Anne." She put her hands on her hips and swayed.

"Stop dancing. It's too early."

"Anne, please." She grabbed my shoulder and jostled me. "Get up."

"Why didn't you get this before? Nothing's open on Christmas."

"Everything so busy. I have to do so much." My mother was president of the church. She shook her head. "I forget."

My parents didn't have a computer, so I couldn't steal the song online like a normal person. I ended up driving all over the Valley looking for an open record store. Everything was closed, either permanently or just for the holiday. It was possible that a bunch of Korean seniors were going to miss out on the Macarena. So in that sense, I'd saved their Christmas. Then I found an open store. I charged in. It was empty, save one employee.

"I need that 'Macarena' song. Do you have it?"

"Uh . . . probably?"

"It's for my mother, I swear."

"Sure. I believe you."

He handed me a CD.

"Wait, this is *twenty* dollars? For five songs?"

"It's an import. It's the only one we have."

"Import from where? You should be paying me to take this."

The song is about a girl, named Macarena, who spreads happiness to the world around her, via her pants. She dreams of moving to New York and seducing men. It is the perfect song for church. It's by Los del Rio, a "musical" duo of men who are very north of middle age. They are an impossible shade of tan; they look like rotisserie chicken. Like Picasso, Penélope Cruz, and chorizo, the Macarena is among Spain's finest contributions to our culture.

I went home and put the CD on the stereo for my mother. The speakers blasted the contents of a diaper, refashioned as song and dance. My mother practiced the Macarena in different skirts.

"This one look okay? Maybe I wear pleat skirt? It swing more." She gyrated her hips sensually. I winced. As far as I'm concerned, my parents have only had sex twice.

"The skirt looks fine, Macarena does not."

"*Ayoo,* Anne, you so grump."

She looked at herself in the mirror as she placed her hands one by one on the back of her head and thrust her backside. Then she ran out the door, my dad and Los del Rio in tow. My father most certainly was not going to do the Macarena. I've never seen him dance.

Every December since I was twelve, my mother has helped organize a big Christmas feast for the entire congregation. She plans an extensive menu with other church ladies and always volunteers to make the more challenging dishes. Cooking enough short ribs to feed hundreds of people is an inhumane amount of work, but it comes with great reward: "Everybody say my *galbi* best! Nothing left, all gone!" She's not going to get the glory by making a garden salad; no one remembers lettuce. Plus, my mother would rather eat her own food than someone else's rubbery, underseasoned beef. According to her, there are some ladies who can't be trusted with a spoon, including myself. Whenever I try to cook with her, she hovers and micromanages, then ends up shooing me away so she can do it. I'm not even a bad cook. On Christmas, my mother spends all morning marinating and frying an entire cow, and the smell of oil and garlic permeates the whole house, including the pillows and blankets. This is after she's spent the week putting up decorations at church, picking up poinsettias, and clearing Costco out of chopsticks. Somewhere in all that, my mother rehearses with the choir and helps coordinate the evening's entertainment (if you can call a talent show entertainment).

I find it ironic that my mother works hard organizing her church's holiday festivities, when it was the work that drove her to kill our family's Christmas in the first place. But I can't point that out to her now. Our Christmas has been dead for much too long. I suppose I could resurrect the holiday spirit and persuade my family to get back into it. I could buy a real tree, along with lights and decorations. I could put up stockings and hang wreaths on the grilles of everyone's cars. I could convince my brother to roast some meat and I could bake sugar cookies, which my parents wouldn't like because they prefer the savory to the sweet. I could do all these things, sure, but this is too much work, and the irony of that isn't lost on me.

What is lost on me is my parents' insistence that I fly home for the holidays, even though we don't do anything. Every December, I buy a plane ticket that's a latte short of $500, and every December, I ask myself the same thing: Why fly to L.A. when I can fly to London for the same price? Wouldn't I rather be drinking a pint and eating crisps and making fun of British teeth? Why, yes, yes I would. But I never do this. Instead, I fly on Christmas afternoon when it's relatively cheaper. I eat a tired, soggy hummus sandwich from the only lunch counter open at JFK and get delayed on the tarmac. It's a holiday tradition.

Several years ago, when my parents were about to move, I flew back to pack up my stuff. If there's one lesson I've learned from living in a postage stamp of a studio, it is this: Objects never love you back. All they do is take up space, physically and mentally. I threw everything away without hesitation or remorse—friendship bracelets, childhood drawings, mix tapes, favorite dolls. Still, I spent an entire week at home cleaning out my old bedroom and helping my parents. Then, two months later, it was Christmastime.

"I think I'll stay in New York this time."

"What?" My mother choked on something. Anger, perhaps. "Anne. No."

"Why? I *just* saw you guys. Didn't you have enough?"

"Never enough to see our only daughter."

"But I'll save money." I could buy a plane ticket, or I could buy four pairs of shoes or help send a kid to college. Clown college, even.

"Christmas not when you save money. What you do then? What is better than visiting you mommy and daddy?"

"Are you sure you want me to answer that?"

"What about Grandma? She die soon."

"Woman, please." My grandmother went to the gym nearly every day to aerobicize in the pool. "I can come in February. I'm sure everyone will still be alive. Tickets will be half the price."

"Anne. You have to come. It Christmas."

"But we don't do anything."

"Doesn't matter. Christmas for family, remember?"

On Christmas, I flew to Los Angeles with an old friend from high school. He's Jewish, but his family comes together for

Christmas anyway, because it's Christmas and that's what people do. His mother picked us up and dropped me off at my parents' new house. It was the first time I'd been there; I hadn't gotten to see it on my last visit. The house looked exactly like all the other houses on the street, two stories with beige stucco, a gray roof, and a white garage door. It wasn't particularly big or small, just serviceable. There was a tiny patch of a front lawn and some kind of bush. That's it. The house had no personality, no distinct feature that could complete this sentence: It's the one on the right with the _____. Our old house had a lot of charm—a one-story "California-style ranch" with a clay tile roof. The house was shaped like a U and set back from the street, mostly hidden by ancient oaks. For a while, an owl had taken up a tree as its home. A brick path lined with purple pansies and honeysuckle shrubs led up to the front door. Even the spigots in the yard were quaint—little brass woodland creatures. My favorite was a fat toad, complete with adorable warts. I was disappointed that my parents had downsized to such a lackluster box in an even more lackluster tract-housing development. I had to remind myself that it's what's on the inside that counts. The house would have our furniture and our Catholic tchotchkes and my family, and it would still feel like home, or at least a version of it.

The house was dark and quiet. I knocked on the door and no one answered. I knocked again loudly.

"Hey, it's me!"

I tried the doorknob and it opened easily. Our family has never locked the doors; nor did any of my friends' families. You just knocked and let yourself in and no one would be surprised to see you, as if you just belonged there. At first I thought I had entered the wrong house, but then I saw my second-grade school portrait—me with pigtails and enormous front teeth hanging over my bottom lip. I looked around. There was disassembled furniture, opened boxes, and an ocean of bubble wrap, which would eventually end up in the ocean. My parents had moved in a month ago, but it looked like little progress had been made.

"Hello? I'm home!"

The house was silent, save the hum of the refrigerator. Normally our house is filled with noise—people bickering, dishes clinking, K-pop stars popping. There was a creepy air to the place, as if at any moment there'd be a knife to my throat, and I'd be thrown in the basement, though houses in California don't have them. Maybe I'd be shoved in the laundry room. I'd see my parents tied to a chair, and my mother would be eating her way out of her gag. My father would sit there silently, tracking and criticizing all the mistakes the thieves were making—those amateurs. The burglars would quickly realize my parents don't have nice things and they'd consider taking the plastic statuette of the Virgin Mary just for its kitsch. Finally, they'd take the candlesticks and haul ass, only to discover that they're gold-plated.

"Mom? Dad?"

I checked the kitchen. Preparing Korean food requires a lot of space since each meal has half a dozen side dishes. My mother had always complained about the size of her kitchen. This new one was half the size, with an ineffectual strip of counter space. I could already sense her frustration; there were pots, pans, and jars of fermenting something on the beige tile floor. But other than that, the kitchen was empty.

"Where are you guys?"

I navigated through a maze of boxes and went upstairs to the master bedroom; maybe my parents were getting dressed for church and hadn't heard me come in. I peeked into their bathroom. His-and-hers sinks, but there was no sign of him or her.

I reached for my phone and called my mother.

"Anne! You get in house okay? How you like?"

I heard laughter and commotion in the background.

"House looks . . . great. Are you at church still?"

"No, no, Mommy in Las Vegas!"

"WHAT?"

"I drive you aunt, uncle, and grandma to Las Vegas. You aunt never go before."

"Are you kidding me? It's *Christmas*."

"Why so surprise? I tell you we go."

"No, you didn't."

"Yes, I did."

"No, you most certainly did not. Why else would I be surprised?"

"Maybe you forgot."

"Maybe you forgot to tell me." I choked my phone. "Why would you go to Las Vegas?"

"For fun. Why else people go? We see Caesar Palace and New York–New York hotel and—"

"Oh, New York, I'm familiar with that place. Because I just flew from there. I meant why would you go to Las Vegas if *I'm* in Los Angeles? When are you coming back?"

I heard ringing and whirring and ka-chinging. My uncle was whooping and laughing. My mother chatted excitedly with my aunt. They were trying to figure out how to play a slot machine, as if that's something you need to figure out. You just put coins in and pull the lever. Then you lose money and do it again.

"Hello, pay attention to me."

"Maybe January second? Not sure. You aunt never see Hoover Dam, so maybe we go and she can see and everyone be happy."

"Yes, everyone is happy. Big family trip," I growled. "Wait, you know I leave before then, right?"

"Okay, merry Christmas, I call later, bye." She hung up.

I pounded the keypad on my phone. "Dad. Where are you?"

"Where else? I'm at lab, I have lot of work."

"Who works on Christmas?"

"I have big deadline. Very, very busy. I go to San Jose to see client day after tomorrow. No time. You mommy went to Las Vegas."

"No one told me."

"We tell you. I come home late, don't wait for me, okay?"

"Why would I ever wait for anyone on Christmas?" I rolled my eyes. "I should've just stayed home."

"No, you have to be home for Christmas."

"Dad, you're not even home for Christmas."

"But I'm here!"

"That makes no sense. I'm going to call Mike."

"Oh. You not talk to Mike yet?" My father paused. "You should call him."

I smashed more buttons on my phone.

"Yo, what's up, dude? I'm in San Diego."

"What? Are you kidding me?" I ripped off a piece of packing tape stuck to my jeans.

"Didn't Mom tell you? Where are you?"

"I'm in L.A. Didn't you know I was coming?"

"No one told me."

I sighed. "But I always come on Christmas."

"I thought you'd stay in New York since Mom went to Vegas. Wait, you know Mom went to Vegas, right?"

In a family of people who have a lot to say, they never say what you need to know. I made my way to the kitchen. I was hungry. Whenever I visit, my mother makes sure I'm well fed, even though

I can cook for myself. She prepares all my favorites and tests new dishes for me to try. If she leaves the house before I'm awake, she sets the table with breakfast, which, in terms of Korean food, is identical to lunch or dinner. It's one of my favorite aspects of Korean cuisine; I can live without the flavorless snoozefest that is scrambled eggs and pancakes. If my mother will be gone for the whole day, she'll leave directions for meals and explain where to find specific containers and vegetables in the refrigerator. I looked over at the kitchen table. There was a pile of mail, but no food and no note.

I opened the refrigerator expecting to find food, since that is what one would find in a refrigerator, but it was empty. Well, not exactly. There was a loaf of bread, an institutional tub of margarine, and Styrofoam trays of raw beef. There was also half an onion and a carton of French vanilla Coffee-Mate. I'd never seen my parents' refrigerator so bare. Usually it was so stuffed you couldn't see the back. Stacks of Tupperware would block the lightbulb, so it'd be dim inside—finding anything was a challenge. Items would be pushed to the back and forgotten, lending the refrigerator a very memorable odor. It was a happy, first-world problem. But this refrigerator was not so happy.

My belly gurgled and churned. If I don't eat every few hours, I get "hangry," a deadly combination of hungry and angry. My friends have seen a very ugly side of me. I looked in the rice cooker; there's always rice in it. But not this time. My mother once told me it was bad luck to have an empty rice cooker. I guess she was right. I looked in the pantry and found three kinds of flour, a kilo of dried anchovies, and a package of dried seaweed. There was a container of rice, but it would take forty minutes to prepare and I was already in a rage-fueled hunger, or a hunger-fueled rage. I loaded up on slices of sourdough with partially hydrogenated soybean oil and dreamed about my mother's cooking:

glass noodles with vegetables, seasoned burdock root, kimchi and bean-sprout soup. She's famous for her mung-bean pancakes. I've always told my mother she should open an International House of Pancakes that's actually international and show everyone how it's done.

I walked over to the den, a small room lined with mirrored closets. There were more boxes and a TV, an outdated model with bunny ears. I sat on the floor and turned it on, but the reception was horrible. I was watching either *A Christmas Story* or porn. I turned on my laptop so I could broadcast my fury on the Internet and then look at pictures of animals. Have you seen a fennec fox? It's like 80 percent ears. I realized my parents hadn't set up their Internet connection, so I tried to steal the neighbor's. I failed. I think there are two things that should be free for everyone. The first is access to the Internet. The second is toilet paper. All homes should just come with these things, the way they come with walls and a floor. I'm happy to pay for everything else.

I gave up on the computer and yawned. I'm not much of a napper. When I was growing up, there was no time to rest. There was homework, piano lessons, flute lessons, Korean school, Sunday school, extra "Mommy homework," tutoring, track practice, band rehearsals—the list went on. My parents thought naps were wastes of time. Why sleep when you can be studying for the SATs? I've read that naps can help reduce anxiety, hyperactivity, and depression. They can boost visual, motor, and spatial skills; improve memory; heighten creativity; and decrease the risk of heart disease. I often wonder what I'd be like now if I'd slept more when I was younger. Maybe I'd be a Zen monk who'd handcraft Victorian dollhouse furniture. My blood pressure would be 120/80. Napping doesn't come easily to me, so when I'm tired, I just reach for another coffee. However, there was no coffee in the house. Specifically, no coffee I was willing to drink. My father's Sanka is not coffee, nor is my mother's "holiday spice" blend. I'm not sure what holiday spices are exactly—maybe a mélange of disappointment, wrath, and salt. I decided to attempt a nap.

I lugged my suitcase to the extra bedroom and that's when I noticed there was no bed. There was, however, a coffee table. A bedroom without a bed is like a bathroom without a toilet. It's just false advertising. I guessed I would be sleeping on the couch. Except, I couldn't find the couch. I double-checked the living room just in case I'd missed it, as if a couch is something a person can miss.

I jabbed at my phone. "Mom! What am I supposed to sleep on tonight?"

"Where else? You sleep on floor."

"For five days?"

"Korean sleep on floor every day."

"Not if they have beds."

"I think blanket in closet. Maybe in box somewhere."

"Which box?" I looked around. Boxes outnumbered humans a thousand to one. They were unlabeled. My parents can't be bothered with labels. Or children. "Mom?"

My mother was quiet. Maybe she realized how she'd messed up. She'd guilt-tripped her daughter into visiting and then abandoned her to go gambling on Jesus's birthday. Maybe she'd finally apologize for this and, while she was at it, apologize for everything she'd ever done, ever. In high school, I took in a stray cat that slept in my armpit every night. When I left for college, my mother kicked it out of the house without telling me. I never saw him again.

"Hello, Mom?"

I heard the pouring of quarters and whirring. My mother and

her siblings were babbling and laughing. I would've liked to be there, explaining the slots to everyone, losing at blackjack, exploring pawnshops off the Strip. I love pawnshops and their pleasant air of desperation and broken dreams. Dark as it is, I love seeing what people give up. But my mother had never invited me on the trip, or even told me about it. I was simply forgotten. Who forgets a kid? There are government agencies that ensure children aren't neglected and that no child is left behind. It occurred to me that my uncle had also left his kids on Christmas, and my aunt, who lives in Seoul, had escaped to L.A., away from her kids and grandchildren. My mother was right; Christmas is about family, just not all of it. Or even most of it.

I retreated to the den again and plopped myself down on the floor. My grandmother had slept on the floor her entire life. She'd also complained about a sore back her entire life. When I was really little, I'd walk on her back and she'd sigh with relief, and then fall asleep. Then I'd curl up next to her, taking in her warmth and her scent of sour medicinal herbs and White Linen perfume. In the first apartment I had out of college, I slept on a futon mattress on the floor because I couldn't afford the frame, or any other kind of furniture. My friend said it looked like a crack den; all that was missing was a piss-stained corner. And crack.

I was searching for pillows and blankets when I heard a faint beep. At first, I thought it was just my imagination—trauma, be it physical or psychological, can induce phantom sounds. This holiday was certainly traumatic. But then I heard it again. Beep. I sat still for a few seconds, straining to hear. It definitely wasn't my phone; my ringtone is from *The Legend of Zelda* (an actual nerd alert). Beep. I stood up and looked around the den, checking the TV and the VCR. My parents still have—and use—a VCR. Both were off. I began walking around the house. I stood in the hallway, frozen, my head cocked to the side. Beep. The sound could have been anything, from anywhere—a timer on a shelf or an alarm clock inside of a box. Beep. I began searching frantically inside cabinets and drawers. Beep. The sound was driving me crazy. I realized that this is what Mike must feel like.

My brother is mostly deaf in one ear—damage done from a very high fever when he was an infant. When we were kids, I had to go to his room and ask him to do chores or sit down to dinner because he couldn't hear me yelling. Though, maybe he was just ignoring me. Anatomically speaking, we have two ears so we can figure out what direction a sound's coming from and not get killed by tigers attacking from one side. Mike essentially has one good ear. It takes him a while to find a phone that's buzzing or ringing—if he even hears it in the first place. He wouldn't last a minute in the jungle. Neither would I, but for entirely different reasons. I can't survive outside my natural habitat of polluted streets and climate-controlled buildings.

The sound was coming from upstairs. I walked up and down the hallway, pausing every time I heard it. I finally singled it out. It was coming from the master bedroom. It was the smoke detector high above the bed. The battery was running low. A red light was demanding attention and complaining. I could relate. Beep. I groaned. I stood up on the bed and tried to reach the detector, but I was too short—which is more or less the story of my life. Roller coasters eluded me for most of my childhood because of the height requirement of forty-four inches.

I went into the garage to look for a ladder. There was a pile of stuffed garbage bags and a wall of cardboard boxes. I noticed one from my old bedroom. It said THIS SIDE UP with gigantic red arrows. The arrows were facing downward, of course. I'm sure there was a ladder somewhere in the garage, but I couldn't find it.

Beep. I jumped up and down on my parents' bed to pull the smoke detector down but couldn't grasp it. The ceiling sloped up at a sharp angle. Beep. When I was little, I'd scale counters and dressers to grab dishes or books. My mother would catch me in the act and gasp, "No! What if you die?" Death was not something I understood. I only knew that I needed my Tony the Tiger cereal bowl, a gift from my father (Frosted Flakes was our favorite cereal). Eventually, my mother got me a stepstool and I'd drag it from room to room. Beep. I put a chair on top of the bed, but I still couldn't reach. Then I stacked two boxes on top of the chair, but it was too unstable. Beep. I imagined myself toppling over, smashing my head against a wall. I'd end up unconscious on the floor with a broken femur and a dislocated everything. I would die alone, in a pool of blood. Merry Christmas. Beep.

Then I heard another sound. It was coming from somewhere else in the house. Beep. Beep. I traced it to the living room, where the ceilings were a good three feet above me. I guess the batteries in the detectors had been put in at the same time, so they ran low at the same time. Beep. Beep. I tried throwing my shoe at it. I left a dark smudge on the freshly painted ceiling.

And then, another beep.

"Are you kidding me?" I looked around expecting an answer.

This one came from the hallway. Beep. Beep. Beep. I felt like I was in a hospital room full of heart monitors. It was just a matter of time before I flatlined.

I needed to leave; I needed a drink. In that order. I called a friend who was finishing up Christmas dinner with his family.

"Can you pick me up?"

I rolled my suitcase outside and parked it on the driveway. I wasn't sure where I was staying, but there were plenty of couches in the greater Los Angeles area. I looked up and down my parents' street. Christmas lights blinked on all the houses and I could see flickering trees through the windows. One family had gift-wrapped their garage door, complete with a gigantic silver bow. I could hear laughter and music coming softly from the house next door.

I sat down on the lawn, running my fingers through the thick grass. It felt cool and soothing. When I was little, my father taught me how to hold a blade of grass between my fingers and blow on it to make a sound—something akin to a loud, high-pitched fart. I quickly discovered the trick also worked with leaves and explored different pitches and tones. Soon I was performing en-tire symphonies in farts in our backyard, disrupting all animal life, including my mother. Then my father had taught me how to whistle, which my mother warned me would summon child-eating monsters. I stretched my legs out on the lawn and buttoned up my sweater. When had I stopped being the center of my par-ents' universe? Was it the year we stopped our family Christmas celebration? Or was it this year, when my parents said Christmas was for family but lied?

I could hear crickets chirping and cheeping. There are no crickets in New York City and I can't say I ever missed them. From my apartment, you can hear the quiet hum of the city and if you imagine hard enough, it sounds like the ocean, with the occa-sional honking car and woo-hooing drunk. At night, you can hear my neighbor coo at her cat or hear the gentle banging of pots and pans float up the stairwell. You can see my naked neighbor pace while she's on the phone. Even though she has curtains now, she doesn't always use them. I wondered what I'd have been doing if I were in my apartment. Maybe cooking dinner—fried rice and to-mato soup. It's an odd pairing, but they taste great together. When I was young, my mother would make me fried rice and I'd douse it with a ludicrous amount of ketchup—my bowl looked like it was bleeding. Then I'd complain there was too much ketchup, so my mother would add more fried rice to my bowl. Then I'd add more ketchup. We'd keep doing this until I found the perfect balance and eventually I'd finish eating everything. It wasn't until I was an adult that I understood this was how my mother got me to eat more (as a child, I found eating to be taxing and repetitive). I still love fried rice; it's my comfort food. I realized I was a little homesick for New York and longed to cook something I eat when I'm a little homesick for L.A.

I stared at a flashing snowman on a roof across the street. Someone had risked life and limb to put it in a place where snowmen aren't usually found. Actually, snowmen aren't even found in Southern California. I felt a creeping, cool sensation on my ass. I got up immediately and brushed off my jeans, which now had a dark, damp spot on the seat. I cursed myself and debated changing. I heard faint beeps from inside my parents' house. I sighed and sat on my suitcase, the way hitchhikers do, and waited until I saw the headlights of my friend's car.

Dear Babies Everywhere, Ever,

Take a look at your parents. They're the selfless, loving humans who made you. They're the kind of people who remember birthdays and give money to a coworker's fund-raiser. They always bring dessert to a dinner party. They've considered composting. Your parents are good, honest people. But they look like ass. Their faces are puffy and pasty and their eyes are sunken and bloodshot. Their hair is matted and greasy, gray and thinning. Your mom's been wearing the same sweatpants for three months. They're covered in Cheerios. Your dad needs to shave. Both need a shower, I can tell. All of this is your fault. Why must you cry and demand and protest and do things like get hungry?

Your parents love you, do you know that? They fucking love you. They tell me everything about you: what you ate, how long you slept, what you wore. The answers are butternut squash, two hours straight, an AC/DC onesie. Your parents tell me what you like (dogs, car rides) and what you don't like (chickens, car seats). I know when you go to the park, the beach, or Nana's house. I know that you don't really care for Baba, which is cruel because he loves the shit out of you. Right now your parents are posting family photos all over the Internet. Some are so embarrassing that they'll make you regret living—and no, I don't know why everyone's wearing matching vests. You are the wallpaper for their computers and phones. You are their Facebook profile photos. You are the password to their e-mail accounts. They aren't very secure. Each week, your parents send me videos of you smiling, crying, babbling, or cuddling the toys I gave you. I also receive holiday cards "written" by you: "This year I saw my first snow! What am I supposed to do with this stuff?" It's snow, buddy, all you have to do is get used to it.

Sometimes your parents just stare at you while you're sleeping, which sounds creepy but it's not. In college, my friend had a roommate who'd stare at her while she slept. That was actually creepy. Another friend had a roommate who kept dead goldfish. That was creepy too. Also, aromatic. But your parents don't do that, I don't think. They hold you, caress you, snuggle you, bounce you. For six hours a day, maybe more. It's important to note that you're kind of heavy, and you're only getting heavier. Still, your parents strap you on and pace back and forth for 186 hours a month—that's equivalent to more than a week straight. This is because they love you. Also because if they don't do this, you get colicky, which is parent-speak for "acting like a dick."

Feeding you takes a lot of work, but your parents do a good job: acorn squash with apples, peas with mint and brown rice, banana-mango mash. This is organic, gourmet shit. You're eating the food pyramid! You eat better than your parents, who just split a can of Pringles and called it dinner. I remember when they cooked elaborate meals: oil-poached cod, radish salad, a cassoulet. Your parents would take photos of their food just like everyone else and put them on the Internet just like everyone else. Now they're eating potato chips that come in a can. At one point your parents got worried when your poop was "runny" and "sandy." They told me this—why I don't know—and the only advice I had is that you should stop eating sand. What I'm trying to say is that your parents care about the shit that goes into your body, and the shit that comes out.

Babies, your parents have done nothing but love and nurture you. And yet you demand and rage, complain and weep. Your mom, right now, is buying blueberries for you because you love them. Did you know it's winter? Blueberries are $8, and they came all the way from South America to get into your adorably chubby but unappreciative tum-tum. This tiny carton of fruit cost more than beer—something your mom couldn't drink for a long time. Your mother is doing this because she loves you. She deserves respect. So instead of fussing and wailing, think of how you can make this Argentinean-blueberry-buying lady happy. It's actually quite easy—so easy a baby can do it.

First and foremost, you can sleep more. Did you know lions do nothing but chill for twenty hours a day? They spend about two hours a day walking and fifty minutes eating. Scientists timed all of this because they needed a break from building space pods. Lions are badass; they're like sharks, only on land. Be a lion. Pass the fuck out. And do it in long stretches. This will allow your parents to do stuff, like sleep. Do laundry. Maybe they will even have sex with each other.

You can stop being so demanding. Look, everyone knows you're hungry. Someone is making your food. Someone is blowing on it so it's not too hot for your precious little mouth. So just calm down. Sit in this chair that was bought just for you, the one that comes with a big plate. Wait—patiently— for your dad to delicately spoon food into your mouth from a BPA-free container and wipe off your sticky face. Sometimes when you spit up, you look like that scene in *The Exorcist,* which just adds a layer of menace. Please remember to swallow your food—eating works better that way.

Learn to be by yourself. Eventually, when you get older,

no one will leave you alone. No one. They will want you to do things, like make a PowerPoint or fill out an employee self-evaluation form, as if you're going to say something bad about yourself. So take this opportunity to enjoy private time. Think about algebra. Learn Portuguese—*Onde fica a casa de banho? Obrigada!* Ask yourself questions: Would you rather lose your sense of smell or sense of taste? I read that teenagers would rather lose their sense of smell than lose their phones. You will become a teenager at some point. There's nothing anyone can do about that and I'm sorry.

Look at the crap in your bedroom. Ask yourself, do I need all this? The answer is no. Be happy with what you have. Also, be happy with nothing, because you can always use your imagination to entertain yourself. Imagination is free, doesn't take up space, is mostly nontoxic, and you don't have to clean it. It's what people used for a long time. Then some early human child was like, oh yeah, this stick is so awesome I can play with it all day. And some other kid was like, oh, oh, I want a stick too. A fucking stick. Then later, plastic was invented and that pretty much ruined everything, including sea turtles, which are choking on the toys you played with for two minutes. I guess what I'm saying is that the little drum is really annoying and you should stop playing it. Your parents hate it, and I'm sorry I gave it to you.

Babies, stop crying. Life is so awesome for you. People serenade you with blissful songs and celebratory dances and do that thing where they hide their eyes and you're like, *whoa, what the shit!* You get a whole line of gentle, all-natural skincare products that adults should be using but for some reason are just for babies. Soon you will grow up and start walking around. You will tag the couch with a Sharpie. Later you'll get a dog that everyone else will take care of. Then you'll grow even older and light things on fire or stop talking to your bestie for no reason. You will slam doors. Someone will yell at you to turn down your music. You will puke in the streets because of your friends Whiskey and Weed. You will get a flat tire and call your parents even though you are twenty-five years old. You will work at a thankless job and then at a great one. And throughout all this your parents will love you and you will eat a lot of snacks. Cheerios are just the start of a long and fantastic journey through snacks. So stop crying. Enjoy.

Sincerely,
Annie

PS: Yes, your diaper is full. We know. We don't like it any more than you do. Someone is getting to it.

WOMB WITH A VIEW

My mother got a new car last year. It's a nice one, the kind that gets awards from J. D. Power and Associates for its high performance and customer satisfaction. I don't know who J. D. Power is or why anyone should trust him. He's probably some guy with a clipboard standing outside a supermarket. Whoever he is, he likes my mom's ride. It's luxurious, reliable, and sporty, with the sleek curves of a bullet train. It has a monster turbocharged engine that's wasted on my mother—she can't drive fifty-five, just like Sammy Hagar. And thanks to the booming stereo, it sounds like he's shredding in the backseat, which has enough room for his rock squats and high kicks. The car's steering is as sensitive as a poet, and the buttery leather seats have ass warmers, something I didn't know I needed. After someone drives my mother's car, the seat and mirrors magically go back to her settings. Never again will I hear her bellyache, "*Ayoo,* Anne, you leg so short!" as she wrenches the seat back.

Yet, despite all this, I hate my mother's car. I loathe it. It's an abomination to all things with wheels, including Rollerblades, which are bad enough on their own. Her car is the worst thing that's ever happened to me. Worse than the time I saw a guy whip it out in the subway station. I'm talking about his penis here. There is one feature of her car that angers and irritates me so much that I've considered taking the bus. In Los Angeles. In other words, I prefer what is basically a toilet on wheels to my mother's luxury sedan.

The feature in question is the "communication center." It's a system that automatically connects to my mother's cell phone, displays her address book, and directs calls through the car's speakers. The problem with the communication center is that it enables communication. Calls from my mother have more than tripled. She'll call me several times a day, telling me what she bought at the grocery store or how her kimchi turned out. She'll remind me to bring home clothes to dry-clean even though I haven't set plans to come home. Sometimes she'll call me on a Tuesday afternoon, wondering what I'm doing, and I have to explain, once again, that I'm working, which is what I've been doing every Tuesday afternoon since 1998. I realize I should ignore her, but I just know that the one time I send her to voice mail, she'll be in the hospital or her kidnappers will want a ransom. Still, when it comes to her calls, I can, to use my brother's words, "suck it up, grow a pair, and deal—in that fucking order." I end up answering e-mails, cleaning my desk, or putting together to-do lists while my mother goes on about the incredible sale on mackerel. So really, the problem isn't her incessant calls. It's something even more annoying.

Whenever we're in the car together, my mother scrolls through her address book and calls every single relative on speakerphone. This would be pleasant if they asked questions, I answered, and they listened. I understand that this is how conversations work, but this is not something my relatives understand. Instead, I'm held captive in the car, tied down by a seat belt, and poked and prodded and dismissed by my aunts and uncles. There was a movie that came out a while ago where the hero is held hostage in a phone booth and forced to talk to a crazed sniper who seems to know everything about him. The movie is actually called *Phone Booth* and it was made *after* everyone had cell phones. It's an incredibly stupid movie, but I can relate to it.

"SAY HI TO *SAMCHON*." My mother will never understand that when you use speakerphone, you can just use your regular voice. Whenever she calls people in Korea, she yells even louder because Seoul's really far away.

"Hi, *Samchon*." I grip the steering wheel. I'm driving because the safest place in my mother's car is any spot where she's not in the driver's seat. We're sitting in traffic, which is how we spend 78.3 percent of our time together. The rest of the time we're looking for parking.

"HI, ANNIE, HOW ARE YOU?" My uncle yells at me in Korean; he has speakerphone in his car too. My *samchon* has a furniture store downtown. When I was little, I'd sit at the desks and take notes at imaginary meetings, answer calls on a fake phone, and file papers into a real filing cabinet. I even had a date stamp and an in/out box overflowing with scribbled papers. At the tender age of seven, I aspired to be a temp. I'd like to go back in time and talk to myself: *Look, kid, one day all your dreams will come true and you'll work in an office. For the rest of your life. So why don't you pretend to be a cosmonaut or a deep-sea diver or a dragon rancher? Oh, hey, you got a fax.*

"I'm good. And you?" I generally speak to my aunts and uncles in Korean. Their English is worse than my Korean. I have a tendency to slur my words like a drunk getting a tongue piercing. Korean has ten vowels, and the differences are subtle. Proper pronunciation requires a nuanced and delicate tongue. Sometimes my mother has to translate my Korean into Korean.

"YOU FIND A GOOD HUSBAND YET?"

"I'm not looking for one." I try to squeeze the car into the fast lane, which is hardly going fast, just faster.

"WHY NOT? HOW OLD ARE YOU NOW?"

"Thirty-five."

"WOW." My uncle gasps, his horror amplified in surround sound. "YOU HAVE TO HAVE A BABY SOON."

"Thirty-five isn't old." Magazines have decreed that thirty-five is the new twenty-five, but clearly my uncle does not read the same rags as I do.

"YOUR TIME IS RUNNING OUT."

"No, it's not."

My mother nods gravely. "LISTEN TO SAMCHON!"

"Don't worry, I'm listening." I turn down the volume and my mother turns it back up. I glare at her dewy, well-moisturized face, but she doesn't notice because she's too busy dialing someone else.

"SAY HI TO GOMO."

"Hi, Gomo."

It's my aunt on my father's side. One Christmas, she gave me a gigantic jar of peanuts and then asked for the jar back. (It was the perfect size for making kimchi, she explained.) The following year she gave me a laundry bag with the name of their family Laundromat on the side. It's the biggest laundry bag I've ever seen; it could double as a sleeping bag during an apocalypse, be it nuclear or zombie.

"What's wrong, Annie?"

"Nothing's wrong."

"Then why aren't you married with kids?"

My mother smiles smugly.

I shift in my seat and turn down the ass warmer. "Because I don't want marriage and kids."

My mother scowls. "Anne."

My *gomo* laughs. She has a distinct high-pitched, nasal cackle. It's one part crow and two parts dolphin caught in a fishing net. "We'll see, you don't know what's going to happen."

I cough. "But I do know what's *not* going to happen." I change lanes again, deciding that the fast lane is slow, and the slow lane is actually faster. I would like to get home as soon as possible, away from the speakerphone. What I really want is to teleport. How is it that scientists can grow human ears on the back of mice, but they can't zap my molecules and reconstitute them a different location?

My mother pushes another button and browses her address book.

"I think I've had enough calls." I reach over and brush her hand away from the communication center. I miss her old SUV with the torn seats, dinged bumpers, and 250,000-plus miles. The doors wouldn't lock and there was no speakerphone. There weren't even working speakers.

She waves me off and scans her endless list of relatives, friends, friends of friends, and friends of friends of friends who are now her friends. Every Korean from the 818 to the 213 is on there, which is a lot since L.A. is the third-largest city in Korea. "Anne, you have to talk to everyone."

"Why can't we just sit in silence like normal people?"

"SAY HI TO *CHAKUN OHMA*!"

"Why, it's our lovely Annie, how are you?" My *chakun ohma* is my aunt—different from my *gomo*, who is also my aunt. In the States, someone is either an aunt or an uncle. That's it. You have an Aunt Sharon or an Uncle Bob, and it's not obvious to an outsider if they're on your mom's or dad's side. Nor do you care. You just know that Uncle Bob's been married four times—and counting—and maybe he likes beer a little too much. In Korea, each familial relationship has a different label. *Chakun ohma* is the aunt married to your father's younger brother; your father's sister is *gomo*. *Kun eemo* is your mother's older sister, and the aunt married to your mother's brother is *way-seung-mo*. There are separate sets of labels for uncles, cousins, and even spouses of cousins. It'd be easier if we just used people's names, since that's why we have them in the first place, but in Korean culture you never call elder family members by their first names. Meanwhile, my friend Larry, who grew up in Greenwich Village, calls his parents by their first names. I don't even know the names of all my aunts and uncles. I have fourteen of them. And herein lies the true evil of the communication center. If traffic is bad enough—and it always is—my mother will call everyone in my family to badger me and my uterus.

"Hi, *Chakun Ohma*."

"You getting married soon?"

I groan.

"Don't worry, Annie."

"I'm not worried."

"You just have to give it time."

"Really, I'm not worried."

"Sometimes it comes when you least expect it. Then you'll find someone and have lots of beautiful babies together." She pauses and asks my mother, "Did Annie understand all that?"

"No, no, I got it, thank you for being so interested in my—" I stop and let my sentence die. I don't know how to say "nether bits" in Korean. My vocabulary has a lot of holes.

"Yoon-chong still isn't married." My *chakun ohma*'s words are tinged with frustration, shame, and regret. My cousin Yoon-chong is over forty and not married. For twenty years, her single status and desiccating womb were regular topics at family dinners. Eventually everyone gave up on her and placed their attention on the younger, more eligible daughters. Of course, the boys never get this kind of attention; our family is traditional, which is a polite way of saying sexist. My cousin Andy is also over forty and unmarried, but no one seems to care. He spends his time riding his motorcycle and coaching a women's club volleyball team; he swears it's all business and that some of the players are Olympic hopefuls. (Technically, aren't we all Olympic hopefuls? I hope to be on the curling team.) My brother, who's just shy of forty, is more interested in gaming and comic cons than in marriage and babies, and everyone accepts that. But Yoon-chong is a spinster with no prospects because her lady parts are a bleak wasteland that can't support life. Her uterus is like Mercury, which reaches 800 degrees Fahrenheit during the day and –279 degrees Fahrenheit at night. It's an inhospitable world that has no atmosphere.

My mom shakes her head sadly. "Yoon-chong is so smart and talented. What a waste."

I roll my eyes. Marriage and kids aren't Yoon-chong's priority at the moment. She's a successful graphic designer for a major fashion company, but my family doesn't see that. In high school, my physics teacher put a Slinky on a table to demonstrate potential energy. ("It has stored energy. It can do so many things, but it's not doing them at the moment.") My family sees Yoon-chong as a Slinky at rest, just a coil with unfulfilled, wasted potential. "Mom, she's happy. Leave her alone."

On my father's side of the family there are eight of us cousins living in the States. But only two are married and only one has a kid. It's a real family tragedy. After Yoon-chong, there are only two maidens left, Tina and me. Tina is older—she can smell forty's impending, bitter doom. She's an elementary school teacher and is surrounded by kids all day; she's in no rush. I can already feel our aunts and uncles giving up on her. As the youngest at thirty-five, I'm the family's last shot; there's still time for me to get married and spread our genes even farther. If Yoon-chong's womb is like Mercury, then mine is something like Gliese 581d, an exoplanet that's one of the best candidates for habitability outside Earth: It could possibly sustain life, but close observation is necessary. Very close. My family would aim a telescope at my crotch if I'd only let them.

My parents, aunts, and uncles are surrounded by reminders of what they don't have. Their friends have grandkids all over the place, on their phones or in their wallets or on their key chains. On more than one occasion, I've seen grandchildren hanging around rearview mirrors. Whenever my mother and I run errands together, we always bump into her friends, along with two generations of progeny. I hate going to the store with my mother because everything takes twice as long with all her endless yammering and baby pinching. The conversation always ends up on me, specifically my unwed, childless, dire state of existence and the shriveling Turkish apricots I call my ovaries. They see me as a uterus in glasses holding a flashing VACANCY sign.

Sometimes when we're in the car, my mother calls friends on speakerphone just so she can drop fascinating bits of news for my benefit, like how her friend's son, who went to Harvard, married a lawyer and now has a baby. Or how a friend's daughter, who also went to Harvard, married a doctor and now has two kids ("One boy and one girl. How lucky!"). Last year, my mother attended a wedding where the bride (a lawyer) and groom (a doctor) both went to Harvard, and now they are expecting a baby who will no doubt go to Harvard. It's an impressive cycle, one that looks like this:

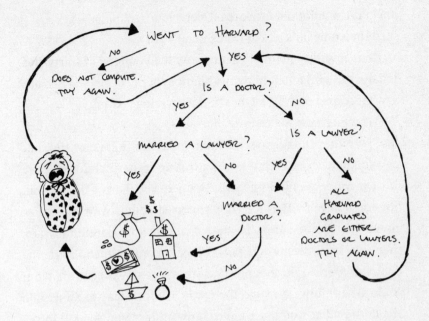

But I know that for every son or daughter who's a neuro-oncologist at Cedars-Sinai, there's a kid who fashions pipes out of Xbox controllers or, worse, wants to be an actor. At Berkeley, there was actually a class on bong building. It combined physics, engineering, and architecture; it was an interdisciplinary course. I was waitlisted and didn't get in.

Once my mother suggested we go to lunch with her friend—and her friend's son. He had graduated from Harvard twice, a feat even Jesus couldn't achieve.

"No. Absolutely not."

"Why? He nice."

"You met him?" I imagined my mother sizing up her friends' sons. Interviewing and vetting them, looking at their transcripts and sperm counts, asking about professional experience and strengths and weaknesses and where do you see yourself in five years? What can you do for us that other candidates can't?

"No." My mother shrugged. "Not yet."

"Then how do you know he's nice?"

"His mommy tell me. He lawyer . . . *for doctor!*" Hearts and dollar signs pirouetted in my mother's eyes.

"Of course he is."

"Just go lunch."

"I'd rather throw myself into a volcano." There's an Indonesian folktale about a couple who, unable to have children, pray to their mountain god for help. The god says, sure, I'll help you, but you'll have to sacrifice your youngest child—your most precious. The couple agrees because that's how desperate they are; then they have twenty-five kids. When it comes time to settle the deal, the couple refuses, and the god gets angry, as gods are wont to do when things don't go their way. He threatens to annihilate the entire village, so the couple throws their youngest kid into a volcano. The lesson learned is that sometimes you literally have to make sacrifices to get what you want. I'd sacrifice myself before getting set up by my mother. My mother would sacrifice me to get a grandchild with a future in medical malpractice. The real winner in all this would be the volcano.

"Anne, just go."

"No."

"Why not?"

"Mother, stay out of my vagina." I walked out the door, got into the car, and drove away. That was ten years ago. She hasn't tried to set me up since.

At an old job, I had a coworker who'd ask the same question over and over again: "Do you think the files can go out tomorrow?"

Then, "How about tomorrow?" followed by, "Maybe they can go out tomorrow?" Later still, "Tomorrow's a good time for everything to go out, right?" He'd keep asking until he got the answer he wanted to hear. This is what my parents, aunts, and uncles do, taking to heart the absurdly entitled adage of "Ask and you shall receive." However, in this case, all the asking will amount to receiving nothing. Specifically, from my uterus.

"Anne, when you marry?"

"I don't want to get married."

"How you know?" My mother looked warily at me. "You never been marry."

"If I don't want kids, why bother getting married?"

"Annie. No." My father cringed, his cheeks, eyes, and mouth twisting into a tight knot. One of my housemates in college had a shirt with a cartoon cow stepping on its own udder. The look on the cow's face was a golden blend of surprise, confusion, and total agony. Underneath the drawing it said, "Uff da!" which is a Norwegian–Minnesotan–North Dakotan interjection that loosely translates to "ugh" or "oy vey." Whenever I see my father cringe, I think of this cow.

"It's not for me. We've been through this. Stop looking so surprised."

"Annie, marriage and baby for everyone." My father dropped his chopsticks on the table. He squinted at me sternly, his beady eyes disappearing between deep wrinkles.

"Did we not have this conversation yesterday?" In fact, we had. "I just don't want kids. You know, there are a lot of people who don't have them."

"Yes, but they very sad." My mother frowned, mourning their loss. "So sad."

"I'm really happy with my life."

"You happy now, but later you wish you had a baby. Then, too late. You regret it." My father shook his head ominously.

"So you have one now."

"I can't just *have* a baby. It's not like I can get one at Costco." I imagined an aisle of infants, between pallets of baby formula and diapers. I suppose babies would come in packs of ten.

"That why you have to look for husband," my mother explained. "Find good one."

I hate when people say you have to "find" a husband or wife, as if you've lost one, like a sock or your virginity. "I don't want to get married."

"You need husband to take care of you," my father explained, "and buy you house."

"I take care of myself, thank you. I'm pretty sure my rent is more than your mortgage."

My mother put a piece of beef in my dad's bowl. "I been saving money for you wedding since you born."

"You have? That's crazy."

"Why?" My father looked up from his beef. "You have to save."

"Sure, and now you've saved money for something awesome. Go to Barcelona."

My mother served me a bowl of soup. "When you baby everyone always say, 'Oh! Oh! You daughter so cute, I want baby just like her.'"

"That's not even a reason to have kids. Polar bears are cute, but I'm not bringing them into my apartment." I felt the sharp pinch of an oncoming headache. "They're the world's largest land carnivores."

Everyone groaned.

"Okay, let's say I get married and have a baby right now—like in an hour—because I might regret not having one tomor-

row. Then tomorrow I realize, oh crap, I don't want this. Then
what?"

"I can raise it." My mother was a little too quick on the response.

"You've got to be kidding me."

"Do I look joke? Mommy do everything!"

My cousin Eun-hee is a few years older than I am and lives in
Korea. She's a concert pianist, a profession my parents believe is
on par with doctors and lawyers. Even though it's not nearly as lu-
crative, classical music is its own currency. Anyone can be a doctor or lawyer if you "study hard and get all A," but being a concert
pianist takes an innate talent. It was clear from a very early age
that Eun-hee had a gift. It was also clear that I did not, though
my mother thought Mrs. Vogel, my piano teacher with impossibly thin lips, could squeeze it out of me. The emotion, nuance,
and mastery my cousin expresses through the piano leave a mark
on people's souls. She can awaken deep memories or inspire you
to be a better person. You'll want to weep over lost loves while
teaching girls to read in Mozambique. Whenever Eun-hee visited
and sat at our piano, the entire house exhaled. Even when she was
practicing the same piece for hours, the music was still fresh; I
could hear new details or subtle changes as her hands danced flu-
idly across the keys. I've caught my mother swaying quietly with
her eyes closed, savoring a moment of real beauty. Whenever I sat
at the piano, the house would gush blood, like that scene from *The
Shining*. My mother's entire face would bulge, red veins cracking
the whites of her eyes, and she'd yell something about tempo and
dynamics and why can't I play more like Eun-hee with her effort-

less grace, instead of sucker-punching the keys until they cry for mercy. Then, while my mother wasn't looking, I'd move the timer I had to set for my practices from one hour to fifty-two minutes.

Eun-hee has built a successful career, teaching students and touring with orchestras around Asia and Europe. She got married and had a son, Yian. She managed to balance family with long re-hearsals, even longer practices, and her teaching schedule. The bar she set when we were kids went even higher, a bar I'd gladly meet if it had a full liquor license and a pinball machine. But then my cous-in's marriage disintegrated, and as these things go, Yian was caught in the middle. Divorce in Korea is historically frowned upon, and while attitudes have changed today, my family is still trapped in an era when men hunted antelope to provide for the family, while womenfolk cooked, cleaned, and sewed tunics with catgut. Eun-hee's bar sank. Her ex-husband ended up in New York, and she stayed in Seoul. The kid, however, ended up in Los Angeles.

At some point, my cousin and her parents decided that Yian should grow up in the States and get an American education. Not because the Korean school system isn't good—Korea's students rank among the highest in math, science, and reading worldwide— but because it's *too* good. Students typically have classes six days a week, with weekend study sessions and supplementary courses at "cram schools." Even pre-K students attend extra language classes. The homework load is demanding, if not abusive, and all-nighters are so common that stores sell special pillows designed to fit over forearms so you can sleep at your desk. (It's something you might find in *SkyMall,* too.) The college entrance examinations are grossly challenging and competitive, and each year the newspapers publish stories about students who committed suicide from the pressure. In my high school, students had to build a napkin holder—and more than one kid failed. I actually went to a good school.

The family wanted Yian to have a better childhood, and that meant sending him to a country where the school system is underfunded, overcrowded, and failing. I guess the idea was that Yian would do well without working too hard, which is a very un-Korean way of thinking. The Korean government recently reduced the official workweek from six to five days, and people were actually complaining about it. The family also decided that raising Yian in the States would be easier on everyone; a less demanding education meant less financial and schedule strain with all the tutoring and extra classes. Yian could've moved to New York to be with his father, but that wasn't an option. My cousin's ex-husband doesn't talk to her or Yian. I'm not sure what happened, but as far as my family is concerned, he was and is a colossal jackass. So several years ago, my aunt and Yian moved to Los Angeles, a city with one of the worst school systems in America. My cousin stayed put in Seoul, as did my uncle, who staved off retirement to work and help support everyone. But while one family split up, another came together. My mother and my *kun eemo* have always been close, so after forty years, they were finally together again, along with their other siblings and their mother.

For weeks after he arrived, Yian kept asking when he'd go back home to his mother and everyone's hearts broke as they explained, hey, cheer up, you're living with Grandma here so you can go to school, hopefully one that doesn't need metal detectors! It was tough for Eun-hee too, but eventually she got used to it, and her calls became less frequent. Now Eun-hee's remarried and Yian's enrolled in a private elementary school in Los Angeles. My *kun eemo* is raising him on her own—not an easy job for a woman in her late sixties. From what I understand, the best thing about being a grandparent is playing with the kid and then going home to your quiet place and passing the fuck out. My aunt, however, is reliving her twenties, but not the fun part with all the Jägermeister.

The whole thing doesn't seem right to me, like most things in my family. Yian could handle a Korean education, like millions of other Korean kids, or Eun-hee could try to get a job in the States, as tough as it is for a classical pianist. Why would you send your kid away when there are options to stay together? The easiest and most callous interpretation is that she's dumped Yian on her mother. When I see Yian act out, it's hard not to let my thoughts wander there. Only recently did I learn that my aunt spent years pressuring Eun-hee to have a kid and finally convinced her.

"Holy shit, you don't have a baby just because someone tells you to. That's wrong."

"Nothing wrong, except you mouth." My mother looked at me, exasperated.

"If someone doesn't want a kid, then they shouldn't have one. The end."

"Of course Eun-hee want baby. *Everybody* want baby. You *kun eemo* promise she take care and raise." My mother nodded as if it was no big deal.

"It sounds like *Kun Eemo* wanted a kid more than Eun-hee."

When my mother and her sister were in high school, my aunt would round up the neighborhood children and invite them back to the house. She'd give them treats and read books to them and play games; she loved kids and she had a lot of love to give. Then my mother would come home and unleash a satanic fury—her face burning, eyes spinning, mouth spitting bile. The house, she'd lecture, was a haven from the outside world, and now every kid in Seoul was there, eating all their snacks (read: her snacks) and breaking their stuff (read: her stuff). She'd throw all those savages out of the house, including my aunt.

"Anne, everyone happy. You *kun eemo* happy, Yian happy, Eun-hee happy. You know who not happy? People with no kid."

"You can't pressure people into having kids. That's not right." I wagged my finger at my mother. "Did anyone think this through? What's going to happen when Yian's in high school? *Kun eemo* will be a thousand years old." I imagined my aunt, deaf and diabetic, with ankles like loaves of olive bread. Yian would be sixteen years old, binge-drinking and setting things on fire while driving.

"Everything be okay, Anne. You worry about yourself and find good husband. Have baby."

"Oh my God, for the last time, no marriage, no babies. You're killing me, woman. I'm going to a nunnery."

"Even nun marry. To God."

Despite the upheaval and untraditional situation, Yian is sweet, funny, and loving. He's all smiles but also mischievous. He can be fussy and whiny and clingy and stubborn; he can be a real jerk. In other words, he's a normal kid. My parents moved my piano, the one I sat at for thousands of hours (minus eight minutes here and there), to my aunt's apartment for Yian. He refuses to play. Eun-hee and I both despised piano when we started, but we were forced to play and eventually learned to love it. Yian no longer takes lessons; my aunt doesn't want to fight him. She's lost the fire that encouraged and drove Eun-hee's talent. I wonder how my cousin feels about this, though there's not much she can do from Seoul. My mother thinks Yian should be forced to play, though no one's asking for her opinion.

My mother and her sister bicker over Yian constantly; sometimes they'll go for a week without talking. My mother says that my *kun eemo* is too soft and doting—an effusive, unstructured, Montessori blob of a parental figure. She lets him do whatever he wants on his precious voyage of self-discovery. My *kun eemo* says my mother is an authoritarian asshole who should get her own grandkid to torture, and in the meantime, she should mind her own matters and stick to golf. I'm paraphrasing. My father diplomatically chooses to stay out of the way, but whenever my mother complains about her sister, he has a certain look that says, *You know, if Yian had stayed in Korea then I wouldn't have to hear this crap. Uff da!* It takes a village to raise a child, but our village is argumentative and bossy. With Eun-hee, I see what my future could be like if I somehow caved in to my family's pressure. There'd be an entire village of fourteen aunts and uncles helicoptering and harassing, albeit in a loving way.

While I don't envision myself having kids or being married, I do want a committed relationship with someone who'll insist on carrying all the grocery bags. I think the reasons why people have kids or don't have them are clear. They bring immense joy, and it's amazing to see a small human grow up and learn the same things you did and make the same mistakes, or different ones. They say funny shit. But kids take a lot of work, responsibility, time, and sacrifice. They'll come into the bathroom while you're having private time and ask you to read a story, and you will. Plenty of my friends have children, and while I love hanging out with them, I know they're not for me. I come home to my quiet studio, with traces of mentally retarding lead paint and no window guards, and I'm happy. Just not wanting kids is enough reason to not have them. But this is impossible for my parents to understand. It's unfathomable that I wouldn't want the things they have, and if everyone wants kids and I don't, then I'm an exception to nature, an outlier. I'm a peculiar organism outside the realm of understanding, like a platypus. It's easier for my parents and the rest of my family to ignore everything and continue having expectations that I'll never meet. Clearly, the family has a problem with unmet expectations—for example, I expect them to be home for Christmas.

I am in the car, as usual, with my mother, as usual. We're driving to the airport. My mother is fussing with the communication center and scrolling through her address book once again.

"SAY HI TO YOU DADDY."

"Hi, Dad."

"Have good flight." He pauses. "Are you still vegetarian?"

"What does that have to do with anything?" I snort. "Yes. Still vegetarian."

"Annie," my father says, sighing, "no one want to live with vegetarian."

My mother burst into laughter and clapped her hands. Bravo, well played.

I scowl. "You both lived with a vegetarian, remember?"

"No, who want to *marry* vegetarian?" my father asks.

I want to pound my head into the steering wheel, veering the car off the road. My mother and I would be fine, walking away without a scratch thanks to the highly rated safety features of her new car. The communication center, however, would fly through the windshield and land somewhere in Pacoima, where it would be tormented by fire ants. "Listen to me. No marriage. No kids."

"You meet someone and you change you mind," my mother assures me.

"Don't you think I'd be with someone who wants the same things as I do?"

"Who want same thing as you?" My mother sniffs. "No one."

I had dated someone for several years, and while we had ups

and downs like any relationship, there was one issue that couldn't be solved. He wanted kids, and I did not; our stories couldn't end in the same place. For a while we both ignored it, but eventually working through other problems became increasingly difficult. How much work do you put into something you know is going to end? Now I'm dating someone who doesn't want marriage or kids. Plus, he's vegetarian. But I'm not ready to introduce him to my parents yet. "Fewer people are having kids now, in the United States *and* in Korea."

"Says who?" My father scoffs over the speakerphone.

"Says the newspaper." I scoff back.

"Which newspaper? Newspaper for people with no kid?" My mother snickers.

"Annie, who take care of you when you old?" my father asks. "Not us. Somebody else."

"I've been taking care of myself just fine."

"You can't do by yourself," he warns me. "Kid take care of parents later in life."

"Dad, are you saying I should have a kid because I'm going to get old one day?"

He pauses. "Yes."

Traditionally in Korean culture, the sixtieth birthday is considered a milestone. Then people started living longer, so while thirty-five is the new twenty-five, seventy is the new sixty. My father recently turned seventy, and he refused to have a *chilsun* celebration with family and friends because "there no grandkid. What point?" My father moped around the house, feeling his age and his mortality and devastating despair. Even my mother thought he was being a bit dramatic. I know that my father worries about my distant future, after he's long gone. Who will change my diaper and recharge my jetpack/scooter? He also sees my less distant future. Who will provide for me? The answer is me. But that's just not enough for my father.

"I'm not having kids just because later I'll need someone to feed me my medicine." I sighed. "Now, would either of you like to discuss how awesome my hair's been looking? Well, guess what? I cut it myself. In other words, I'm *taking care of myself*."

"Anne, baby make you happy. When you young, you make me so happy," my mother says wistfully.

"Oh, so now that I'm older you're not happy anymore?"

Unlike my father, she's less concerned about my distant future filled with bedpans and IV bags that need changing. She'd like a grandchild in order to feel purpose and joy and bask in the pure love that comes from young kids. It's been a long time since I've made a macaroni necklace for her. She'd like to run into friends in the supermarket and whip out pictures of her own grandchild. She'd like to force the kid to practice Chopin's "Minute Waltz" for one hour and assign twenty pages of math worksheets. She'd like to teach the kid all the hot K-pop dance moves, or at least the Macarena. She'd like hugs several times a day, instead of the two she receives from me—once when I arrive and another when I leave.

"Please, stop, both of you."

"We stop when you marry and have kid," my mother said firmly.

"Think about you future, Annie," my father urged.

"*I am.*"

I realize that the poking and prodding will continue until I'm beyond my childbearing years and the VACANCY sign in my womb is swapped for one that says CLOSED FOR BUSINESS. I once asked my cousin Yoon-chong about everyone's invasive probes into her womb. She just shrugged and said, "You get used to it." They'll never understand, she explained, so why fight it? Just ignore it. I could see the wisdom of her advice, but the problem with rolling with the punches is that I actually get punched (in the uterus). If there's one thing I've learned from my parents, it's to always fight back—whether it's against a mugger or a hexagonal table—even if I don't always win.

"SAY HI TO YOU *KUN OHMA!*"

Dear Reader,

I am surrounded by ridiculously kind, supportive, and talented people who have guided me throughout this project. I will attempt to thank everyone here, even though it's impossible.

Heather Lazare edited with a sharp eye, sweating not only the small details but also the big picture. She pushed me to take a step forward or a step back and made sure I didn't step in anything smelly. The brilliant team at Touchstone/Simon & Schuster worked tirelessly and put a lot of trust in this project and me. Douglas Stewart read every single word I wrote for this book. Multiple times. He is a patient and giving agent.

I owe a lot to Aura Davies, Doretta Lau, Rhena Tantisunthorn Refsland, and Sarah Smarsh, who are all great writers and, more importantly, great friends. They read, laughed, and helped me juice the jokes. Micah Calabrese always makes time for me, my bad puns, and "bropen source brogramming." I thank all my incredible friends for their hugs and advice, and I also thank them for the giant salads and whiskey. I appreciate everyone at work who has been so supportive of my "other career," particularly Karina Linch, Mike Watanabe, and Dr. Avraham Kadar. Patricia O'Toole continues to teach me well beyond the classroom, and Perri Pivovar generously took my photo (again and again) while braving Flatbush traffic. I am especially in awe of the brilliant Joseph A. Ziemba, who has given enough love, encouragement, and insight to propel me forever—that's a long time.

My family continues to be the most caring, most aggravating, and most hilarious group of people in my life. I thank all my aunts, uncles, and cousins for their loving patience and support. My mother and father are inspiring creatures who can laugh at themselves as much as they can laugh at me. My brother, Mike, is the only person who understands them as much (or as little) as I do. He also taught me how to curse— obviously, I learned from the best.

Finally, dear reader, I thank you.

Your friend,
Annie Choi

ABOUT THE AUTHOR

Annie Choi is the author of *Happy Birthday or Whatever.* Her writing has appeared in *White Zinfandel, Urban Omnibus,* and *Pidgin* magazine, among others. Her work includes "fauxbituaries" of famous architects, product reviews of a flammable toaster, and a rant about the dire state of an office-building bathroom. She received her BA from the University of California at Berkeley, and her MFA in writing from Columbia University. She loves animals that eat other animals and hates musicals. Choi was born and raised in Los Angeles but now lives in New York. Visit her website at AnnieTown.com.